For Mom and Dad

Mom, You're my greatest supporter and mender of my broken heart. You've shown me there's nothing as strong as the tenderness of a mother's love

Dad, You're the man I measure the other poor fools by. You taught me to honor myself. The world can strip me of everything; but never my character

And for Grammy, who always told me, "You can't make a silk purse out of a sow's ear"

Facebook: The Greatest Passive Aggressive Weapon EVER

Table of Contents

Table of Contents Continued

Facebook: The Greatest Passive Aggressive Weapon EVER

Reconnect with Your Self-Worth and Unfriend Your Fear

When the founders of Facebook came up with a brilliant idea for connecting with friends, they never imagined their web site would become the weapon of choice for passive aggressive people everywhere. But as with every great idea, there are always those who will find a way to abuse it. Of course, extremely passive aggressive people will never admit to doing this, since they usually view themselves as the victims rather than the perpetrators.

I've struggled with an unhealthy attraction to passive aggressive men for most of my life, although thankfully my ex-husband was not among them. When I finally joined the ranks of millions who connect on Facebook, it was only a matter of time before this became another avenue for a passive aggressive man to show me how he *really* felt about me, although his words always said differently. Like millions of others, my feelings became a fatality at the hands of someone who didn't have the guts to tell me the truth in person, but his intentions were made clear with the click of a mouse. It's the perfect venue for those who struggle with face-to-face confrontation. In fact, Facebook could be called I-*Can't*-Face-You-Book.

But this is not an attack on Facebook. And surprisingly, it's not an endless diatribe lambasting those who use it to make their points passive aggressively, although many examples of internet fodder are strewn throughout the book for illustration. It's a tool to help you examine yourself and the reasons why you're attracted to people who aggravate your self-worth issues. We all have those issues. Some of us wear them more visibly on our sleeves and some of us prefer to "hide" them on Facebook. But whether you hide it or flaunt it, we all struggle with issues of low self-worth.

So why do we always gravitate towards people who irritate those sensitive spots of low self-worth? Because they're causing us to visit those areas and heal them, although part of the healing process is usually very painful. Most of us carry old wounds from childhood – or perhaps earlier, and we're always attracted to people who make us revisit those old wounds and essentially go back and heal them as an adult.

How many of us remember getting picked on or teased at some point in childhood? How many of us were never the first one who got picked for a team? And here we are as adults who have convinced ourselves we've outgrown the need to feel popular amongst peers, yet many of us in the "mature" bracket seem to be on a mission to see who can accumulate the most Facebook friends.

Over and over we play out our long-held fears into adulthood, but we're trying to put a different spin on them. The child inside of us is operating at full-speed in the internet world, where manners, compassion, and civility are not as prized as the number of "likes" or the ease at which we can disconnect from people without being confronted with the pain we've caused them. It's like breaking mom's favorite dish and hiding the pieces from her. You never have to take responsibility or acknowledge the disappointment or sadness your actions have created in another human being.

Years ago, a "Dear John" letter was considered the epitome of spineless disregard. Nowadays, a hand-written break-up letter would actually be appreciated for its personalization as well as the time and energy it took the person to write it. With the fancy new cell phones, you don't even need to type all the words out. Just type the first three letters and the phone can guess the rest of the dreaded words. Maybe next year we'll have predict-a-text, where the phone will actually be able to type the whole break-up message for you if you simply hit an "unlike" button.

Does this mean we've turned into a nation of gutless wimpy children who hide behind our screen savers? Not all of us have a fear of confrontation, although many of us have gotten too reliant on electronic communication. In fact, texting can present its own conundrums for those of us who are too wordy. Dueling texts start flying fast and furious, and the order in which they were sent can sometimes get mixed up, communication confused, and feelings hurt. Case in point: My friend and I were meeting for dinner. Here's the string of texts from my end of the phone:

> **Me**: *I may be running a few minutes late if I hit traffic coming from Boulder*
>
> **Him**: *I'll order you a drink. What kind of beer are you drinking?*
>
> **Me**: *Anything light*
>
> **Him**: *You want a shot of Jagermeister to go with it? LOL*
>
> **Me**: *No*
>
> **Me**: *I'll vomit*
>
> **Him**: *Can't wait to see you and give you a big kiss!*

Here's what he got:

> **Him**: *You want a shot of Jagermeister to go with it? LOL*
>
> **Me**: *No*
>
> **Him**: *Can't wait to see you and give you a big kiss!*
>
> **Me**: *I'll vomit*

Sometimes it's not the written words that have gotten mixed up, but we lose the emphasis our voice inflection puts on certain words, and often lose the intended meaning. I told a man I was dating that I'd like him to read the piece I had just written for a newspaper. His response via text message was, "I'm not in the mood for reading your piece." Slam. Or so I thought. Now consider he was trying to be flirtatious and sexually suggestive, with emphasis on *reading*. "I'm not in the mood for *reading* your piece." A lame sexual joke, yes, but certainly not the snub I'd perceived. So the struggle to maintain compassionate, mature human relations gets ever more strained as we continue progressing into the age of electronics.

Whether our miscommunication or lack of communicating clearly is by accident or intended, our space age technology of electronic communication has spawned a whole new breed of dysfunctional people, armed with gadgets that enable their dysfunctional behavior. While this book may not erase any pain you've been caused by accidental texts, misdirected emails, hidden Facebook secrets or blasphemous posts, its purpose is to steer you back into the bowels of your own human psyche. To understand why you have a burning desire to maintain connections with people who treat you as "less-than" is a freeing experience, reserved for the evolved soul who can also understand the issues of the people who are causing the pain. I'm not saying you have to forgive the cheating scumbag who you busted via Facebook, although you'll be happier if you do. I'm saying you'll begin to view them as an indecisive child in the candy store; who doesn't have the guts to have a tough, honest conversation in person. Is that the kind of partner you want? Or is that the kind of partner you're always attracted to, because subconsciously you feel you don't deserve anything better, or because they force you to confront unpleasant self-worth issues? Once you confront them, can you heal them? Yes, but at times you may feel like a recovering drug addict, dying for a shot of passive aggression or a dose of disregard from a cavalier drug dealer. Maybe it's control you're addicted to, or perhaps a feeling of powerlessness. We all have our version of crack cocaine. We crave the kind of people who are bad for us.

I'm happy to report that I've not only cured my own addiction to passive aggression, but I actually enlisted the aid of some passive aggressive ex-boyfriends to give me examples of their recent antics, and remind me of things they did when we were dating. Yes, we can all laugh about our issues. They know they're passive aggressive, and I know I was addicted to their behavior. But they're good guys! Believe it or not, I've even forgiven the ones who cheated on me. Passive aggression is based on fear, and I feel sorry for anyone whose relationships are affected by their fear. My own addiction to their behavior was based on *my* fear: Fear of being unworthy. And this is the common fear that we must frequently confront in our new age of computerized passive aggression and aggressive aggression.

Facebook Foibles

Find your inner child! Join Facebook and explore what millions have already discovered: the mature person's trick to behaving immaturely. Let's first take a look at some common horror stories from Facebook.

Offender #1: The Unfriender

In earlier days, if we didn't care for someone's personality, we simply avoided them. If someone did something that offended us, we silently vowed to steer clear of them, and it was all done in the most polite version of avoidance that we could muster. Nobody's feelings got hurt from a visible snub. In fact, most people don't have the courage to be blatantly rude in person. But "unfriending" doesn't take courage. It's a silent dagger that's wielded while no one is watching. It's quietly but aggressively showing someone you're no longer their friend, but without any verbal explanation. No need for The Unfriender to deal with conflict. Just an easy cowardly way of slicing a gaping wound into someone else's ego.

Offender #2: The Slanderous Poster

Rather than confronting you, these frequent "posters" use their status update column to slam everyone who has ever wronged them, considered wronging them, inadvertently wronged them, or just breathed the wrong way. The Slanderous Poster is outwardly aggressive, but certainly not passive. Their ire is boldly spelled out in black and white.

Offender #3: The Hider

This person keeps hurtful secrets, posts the evidence, but then "hides" the evidence from those who would be hurt by the truth. These people live in a land of make believe, and they secretly get a rush from the idea of "almost getting caught" in the double lives they're leading. What they fail to realize is that no matter how frantically you try to cover your tracks, you always leave an imprint. There is always someone who has photos or other evidence of where you've been, and the truth will always come to light eventually. The innocent or betrayed will always find out about your secrets and get hurt from your deception, and the one thing The Hider is trying desperately to protect will become tarnished: their own image.

Offender #4: The Shameless Self-Promoter

Home burglars everywhere are rejoicing. The Shameless Self-Promoter publicly posts a minute-by-minute update on their daily whereabouts, thereby affording the public common knowledge of where they are at, where they are going, and who they are with. While the rest of us do not care to know how busy their social agenda is or how popular they seem to be, they're putting themselves in danger by allowing anyone and everyone to track their whereabouts. This person is the master of self-taken cell phone pictures. The Shameless Self-Promoter "checks in" to every place they visit and this act of "checking in" appears to be prioritized over the act of actually enjoying the places they're visiting and the people they're visiting with. After all, if you're having a great time with the people you're with at the places you're at, is a Facebook post the first thing on your mind of things to do? Just as in junior high school, the Self-Promoters want to give others the impression that their lives are terribly exciting, and therefore others will be jealous. They have a burning desire to elicit envy in others. This is the grown-up version of "my toy is bigger than your toy." The Shameless Self-Promoter struggles so much with their own self-image, they're driven to work overtime attempting to craft a different image.

Some of us are in businesses where we are urged to shamelessly promote our products, services, or publicity campaigns on our personal web pages and every other form of social media. Being one of those people, I understand the promotional aspect of business related postings, and I enjoy staying abreast of my friends' campaigns. I also love viewing all the pretty vacation photos and happy faces when friends and family get together. That's what a Facebook wall is for. But The Shameless Self-Promoter is different. They appear to go to several different places every single night, just for the purpose of "checking in." They post self-taken photos so often that you begin to wonder if they are really checking in with the friends they claim to be with, or just popping in the doors of various clubs to take their own picture. Their favorite picture-taking locale, however, appears to be their own bathroom. Self-Promoters never miss a chance at a photo-op in front of their rear-view mirrors either.

Offender #5: The Play-by-Play Putz

These people live on Facebook. 100% of their waking hours are spent documenting a personal diary on their wall. They don't have the anger of a passive-aggressive person, but their lives appear to be spent in passivity, wryly commenting on the aggravations of life. They're friendly folks and they mean no harm to anyone, but they're such an important presence in the Facebook world, they demanded inclusion in this list. (After all, if I didn't include them, they would surely include themselves with a comment or five.) They differ from Shameless Self-Promoters in the fact that they don't have to be going anywhere with anyone to continually post updates. In fact, most of their updates are just private musings that occurred to them while they were watching television, eating cereal, petting the cat, staring at the walls. They don't live terribly exciting lives, but they log a constantly updated journal of their mundane daily activities, and you begin to feel as if you're riding along in their front pocket listening to their mumbled narration of life.

The Play-by-Play Putz is another one who would make a private investigator's life easy. The exact whereabouts of The Putz are always clearly documented on Facebook, as they comment on the absurdities of life that's going on around them. They're the star of their own show. I often wonder if they are really posting messages for others to read, or do they just enjoy keeping an electronic diary?

A day in the life of Putz:

> *1 minute ago: Wow, when did the gas prices go up again?*

> *18 minutes ago: Heading to work and hope I've got washer fluid*

> *31 minutes ago: Wet socks. Thanks dog*

> *37 minutes ago: My dog decided it was a good idea to knock over his water dish*

> *48 minutes ago: Yum orange juice*

> *1 hour ago: Don't wanna get up this morning*

> *9 hours ago: Good night all. Think I'll turn the heat up*

Offender #6:   The Inspirational Quoting Hatchet Murderer

Here's a typical post of The Hatchet Wielder:

> *4 Hours ago near Dallas, TX: "True friends are like diamonds; Precious but rare. False friends are like autumn leaves, found everywhere." – Wise Anonymous Person*

These people manage to find an inspirational quote that cleverly ties in with every situation that offends their ego, and they can effectively slide in their own daggers under the guise of inspirational wisdom. They can always find a quote that is a thinly veiled attack on whoever inspired their angry inspiration. They're the ones who post quotes like, "True friends stab you in the front," by Oscar Wilde. Or, "Sometimes your best friend is your worst enemy." Everyone in their friend network immediately knows something went down with another friend, and a flurry of private messages ensue in efforts to get the low-down from The Inspirational Quoting Hatchet Murderer's mouth in "privacy."   Naturally, The Hatchet Murderer never publicly names names. That would be in poor taste, and they are clearly an echelon above that type of immaturity, as evidenced by their sage inspirational quotes. Though their words can have poetically sharp precision, their cruel intentions can hack you up like a dull blade.

Offender #7: The Untagger

Sometimes The Hider and The Untagger are split personalities in one person. They both wear the same smiling face of the passive aggressive person, but they have different functions. While The Hider tries to keep certain things hidden from certain people, The Untagger doesn't want any incriminating photos on their wall and they don't want *anyone* to know they were in the vicinity of certain people. The Untagger is very status conscious and they don't want to be seen with anyone uncool. They may also be two-timers and they don't want the numerous people they're dating to come face-to-face on their Facebook wall.

The Untagger always hopes that no one noticed the untagging. They silently sever their link to the picture, praying the picture slides wordlessly into cyberspace. If you notice the untagging and inquire about it, they'll usually tell you they just hated that picture of themselves.

> *"But it was a great picture of you!"*

> *"No! I hate the way I look in that shot!"*

> *"But everyone else thinks you look just like Brad Pitt in that picture!"*

> *"I know! I'm so tired of everyone telling me I look like Brad Pitt!"*

The Untagger breathed a huge sigh of relief when Facebook came up with an option that lets you review any pictures you're tagged in before they're posted on your own Facebook. They can now safely snub people before the people's pictures ever appear on The Untagger's wall.

Offender #8: The Blocker

Blocking was designed as a safety method to ensure its members were not harassed by stalkers or crazy people who wanted to bother them. The Blocker discovered its real beauty lied in being another passive aggressive way to deal somebody a silent but deadly blow to their ego. It's the quiet way of saying, "I hate you."

Why Did We Stop Evolving With Evolving Technology?

The number of times that Facebook is cited in divorce court appears to validate the fact that adults have become emotionally invested in their social network and the importance of defining themselves in it. Facebook walls are the new equivalent of bathroom walls full of graffiti. Lawyers bicker and leverage their client's proprietorship over those walls surrounding personal sewage. Rather than fighting over custody of children and pets, people are fighting for sole custody of "friends" who probably don't care if their friendship status is retained or not. But it's a power struggle as well as a popularity contest, all in the name of protecting privacy for the individuals involved. If privacy was the utmost concern, would the parties be airing their dirty laundry in a social media network?

The race to acquire cutting edge technology appears to have slowed the progression of the individual's ascension as an evolving soul. When did we stop applauding wisdom and maturity and start defining humans – including ourselves – as worthy individuals based on social media aptitude? At what point did we lose the human element of personal interaction and begin relying on impersonal non-verbal contact to communicate?

It's not the technology that has turned us into an uncompassionate species. It's the fact that our computers and cell phones have made it easy for the fearful to avoid facing their fears. It's the technology that has enabled us to become lazy and avoid doing the inner work that's required to grow up and evolve, instead of being controlled by our fear. The greatest fear of all is the fear of being found unworthy. Those who suffer from low self-worth issues just discovered an artificial means of attempting to elevate their self-esteem.

The ease at which a passive aggressive person can exercise their unhealthy manner of communicating their feelings just became easier. Ambiguous texts and emails can be carefully crafted since they are lacking in the spontaneity of real conversation. Self-image is built on the screen of a computer, rather than from within. It's not technology's fault, and certainly not Facebook's. It's our own laziness. It's the human penchant for avoiding our own issues, and all issues seem to begin and end with self-worth.

Can you find your self-worth on the web? Of course not, but why don't we teach that in school? Why do we offer children classes that teach them how to find the distance between two points, but we do not offer kids lessons in finding their own value as a human being? The greatest lesson is learned through trial and error throughout our lives; the discovery of self-worth and self-love comes to most of us after years of painful experience grappling with our own image of ourselves. We like to talk about finding our self-worth, but we don't bother trying to give our kids instructions on it. Perhaps that's because we haven't figured out how to do it ourselves.

For the evolved souls among us, self-love has haltingly come in small measures that are equally proportionate to one's forgiveness and acceptance of others. We cannot embrace our own individuality if we don't embrace differences in others. We can't be forgiven if we are not forgiving. And we can't feel worthy of love and compassion if we are not a source of those things ourselves.

So where do we begin in the journey to self-love? Let's begin at a common point of derailment: Facebook.

One Giant Step into Adulthood

I have a challenge for you. If you've been engaged in silent Facebook wars, post an apology to all who have been hurt by your previous postings. Too extreme for you? Then how about this: Post something in your status column to this effect, "Please feel free to post anything on my wall that can be viewed and enjoyed by everyone. Let's be Facebook friendly. Karma's a bitch." Too public for you? Then consider just making a promise to yourself that you will never again use social media to post something that will cause someone else discomfort or pain. Karma *is* a bitch.

If you take one baby step into calling an invisible truce with all your detractors or competitors, you will be amazed at how good you will suddenly feel about yourself. Being the bigger person always has its own rewards, and they're usually internal. When you extend an olive branch of humility and compassion, it's like giving a warm and fuzzy gift to yourself. Your own self-esteem is miraculously elevated by degrees, and you're suddenly free of the constricting shackles of emotional immaturity. You're free to be an adult, a free spirit who is no longer consumed by one-upmanship, getting even, jealousy, or fear. You will actually feel proud of yourself, and that's what self-worth is all about.

Secondly, let's take a look at all those self-worth issues that motivate your unconstructive interactions with others.

"The true test of a man's character is what he does when no one is watching." – John Wooden

The current day psychology seems to be, "A man's character is defined in his profile and validated by the number of views and likes he receives."

Our modern social networking tools challenge us to succinctly describe ourselves in one paragraph or less. Whether it's professional networking sites, dating web sites, or personal web pages, we struggle to put ourselves and our character into sound bites. We're continually creating profiles for ourselves for one reason or another. We're initially uncomfortable when presented with the task of creating a self-advertisement, but we quickly become skilled at marketing ourselves. We're like a bunch of used car salesmen; pointing out our surface appeal while neglecting to take a closer look under our own hoods.

What's under your hood? Jealousy? Resentment? Greed? Low self-esteem? Overall feeling of unworthiness? This appears to be the case with a large portion of our society, judging by the way we subconsciously advertise our insecurities.

Do we really feel we are valuable human beings because of the number of degrees we've obtained, or wealth we've accumulated, or pictures we've posted attesting to our popularity? Do we think our true value increases with our ever-expanding social network? What makes us valuable?

If you took an informal poll and asked people to identify stellar human character qualities, you would garner a list that contained some or all of the following:

> *Compassion, Kindness, Courage, Honesty, Integrity, Loyalty, Forgiveness, Benevolence, Humility, Ownership, Honor, Trustworthiness, Sincerity, Respectfulness, Consideration, Thoughtfulness, and Friendliness*

You surely can observe many or all of these character qualities in yourself, and yet many of us are consumed by insecurities and self-doubt. We never cut ourselves the same breaks that we allow others. We forgive our friends for inconsiderate remarks because we know they are inherently kind. But we overlook our own kind nature because we don't deem ourselves socially desirable or exciting enough. We disregard and devalue our own stellar human character qualities, because we've been conditioned to believe "nice guys finish last." In effect, we sabotage ourselves in our efforts to create a false image of ourselves that we believe will look more appealing to others. And in childish fashion, we resort to behavior that erodes the self-worth of others, hoping it will boost our own self-confidence. We lie, we cheat, we betray, we belittle, we slander in futile attempts to promote ourselves. But the lying and cheating and slandering only make us feel worse about ourselves. Rather than pride, we feel a deserved sense of shame. We may fool others with our carefully crafted image of illusion, but we never fool ourselves. A man or woman's true character is contained within their heart, and only our conscience knows what that true character looks like, although our behavior gives others telling glimpses.

The following is a short list of common manifestations of low self-worth which regularly appear online:

Jealousy: This erodes our self-worth from the inside out, like battery acid. When we feel jealous of another person, we have privately determined their situation is more enviable than ours, and we perceive ourselves as "less-than." We'd like to be in their shoes, with their profile and their pictures and their friends. The human tendency is to overcompensate. Instead of owning up to our envy, we go overboard trying to make *our* life look enviable.

It's quite comical to see jealousy played out on Facebook. People who seldom post will suddenly become hourly Self-Promoters after they've been jilted. In their hasty attempts to make their situation look enviable, they're pathetically broadcasting their own jealousy. They often post thinly veiled criticisms directed at their ex-lover's new flame; the object of their jealousy.

One of my friends ended her relationship with a younger man and took up with a man who was ten years her senior. The younger man suddenly began posting pictures of himself that were worthy of a muscle magazine, with posts that were clearly designed to insult the older man who did not spend hours sculpting his physique, although they were "disguised" as general observations about the aging population. These postings only made the younger man appear even more immature and quite obviously jealous, which was a backfire of his intentions.

Jealousy also takes the form of stalking. Many wasted hours are spent by Jealous people who stalk the pages of those they envy. If they utilized the time spent stalking to work on their own self-esteem issues instead, they wouldn't feel that burning envy that drives them to stalk in the first place.

Anger: All of us feel angry from time to time, but some of us have anger issues that transcend the norm. If you're feeling angry at the world at large, you're sliding into victimhood at a rapid pace. Angry people usually don't pull any punches in social media. Their anger prohibits it. There are no "thinly veiled insults" in the Angry person's repertoire. They just blast their angry comments out in typical blow-horn fashion. Like angry traffic cops screaming through a megaphone at absent-minded motorists, the Angry Facebooker yells with minimal words and maximum exclamation points.

"NEVER GET MARRIED!!!!!!!!!!!!!!!!!!!!!!!!!!!!!!!!"

Their posts have "victim" stamped all over them, and they're repelling those who they could otherwise look to for support. Nobody likes a victim. But everybody hates an *angry* victim.

Superiority: The ultimate in overcompensation, the folks who act snobbishly superior to everyone are in a word, annoying. It may be religious "holier than thou" superiority, or it may simply be status-driven or intellectual snobbery. Either way, it annoys the hell out of everyone subjected to their constant feed of snobbish remarks, and the Superior poster never elicits the admiration they're craving with their superior posts. Their snobbery, designed to elevate their self-esteem, causes others to actually frown upon them and avoid their friendship. The Superior person usually knows loneliness up close and personal. And loneliness is not conducive to healthy self-esteem and self-worth.

Desperate for Approval: Even more annoying if it wasn't outright pathetic. These folks are so transparent in their desire for approval; they begin feeling like an albatross of clinging insecurity to their contacts. They often spend 95% of their waking hours on Facebook. They immediately post a self-effacing comment onto any new activity in their friends' feed. If their friend posted a link advocating euthanasia for all pets over 10 years old, they would immediately agree that their longtime companion, Old Yeller, must be put down. The only opinion they will firmly stand by is their low opinion of themselves. They don't believe in themselves enough to stand up for their own beliefs. They're an animated version of the famous Wayne's World line, "I'm not worthy."

Desperate for Attention: A close cousin of Desperate for Approval, the Attention seekers often drop curious little nuggets that beg for elaboration. You don't need to approve of them, as long as you respond. They frequently invoke song lyrics to allude to something they want you to ask about. Their posts range from, "Sorry seems to be the hardest word," to "Love is a battlefield," to "Never again....(sigh)...." Sometimes they ask open-ended questions. "Do I have a target on my forehead?" "Are all women crazy?" They try to entice us to prod them for the details. "Did the cashier at Starbucks really need to add *that* to my drink?" "Can someone explain why a man would bleach a triangle in his chest hair?" The Desperate for Attention posters could make a nice living in advertising, composing one-line teasers that grab attention. However, their repeated attempts at getting attention get stale very quickly, and they find themselves getting ignored instead. Another backfire.

Identifying Your Own Issues

Looking back on all my failed romantic relationships with men who were completely different from one another, I realized there was only one common denominator: Me. I was obviously attracted to men who weren't healthy for me, so the underlying issues were my own. In attempting to identify my issues, I realized a large percentage of these men did have one common behavior: Passive Aggression. Passive aggression is described as non-verbal aggression that allows a person who is uncomfortable being outwardly assertive or aggressive to passively get what they want. Men are more notorious for this type of behavior, but women can be culprits as well. We all resort to passive aggressive tactics at times, even if in a mild form. Dealing with friends, lovers, or spouses who demonstrate pronounced passive aggressive behavior can be frustrating at the least, and abusive at the worst.

While I could easily identify severe instances of abusive passive aggression, I apparently wore rose colored glasses when dealing with men who manifested a lesser degree of this behavior. These are the people who tell you what you want to hear just to pacify you, but in the end, they will always end up doing what *they* want to do. They will pay lip service to compromising, but their actions never back up their words. They routinely forget agreements and promises they've made. They fail to follow through with plans, and yet they view themselves as the victims if you take them to task. They stonewall, but they may do it in such a charming manner that you readily forgive them. They will use ambiguous statements to avoid being straight with you, and it becomes a frustrating exercise in fruitless attempts to decipher their true intentions. All the passive aggressive men I loved were skilled wordsmiths.

I considered titling this book: Texting: The Greatest Passive Aggressive Weapon EVER, because the whole text messaging system could have been invented by someone with passive aggressive tendencies. I abhor communicating via text message, and yet I've had several boyfriends who preferred texting over talking. Big red flag! In fact, they routinely let my phone calls go straight to voicemail, and yet if I sent them a text 30 seconds later, they readily responded with their own text message. From start to finish, the art of texting has every base covered for a passive aggressive person.

- Timed response to *your* texts, or responding in *their* own time (i.e. when they are good and ready, which is generally after they have had ample time to craft an ingeniously ambiguous response) They will usually tell you they didn't see your text when it came, and naturally you can't argue with that. It may take hours to receive a response; it may take days or weeks. They may tell you you're important to them, but they *show* you that you are not a priority. They may agree to certain circumstances, but their actions will ensure they get things the way *they* want. It's impossible to make a concrete plan with them, due to the time delay they always impose which allows them to be in control, while you're impatiently tapping your heels awaiting their response. Here's an example:

> *3:34 p.m.* **Mary**: *Do you still want to get together this evening? Your turn to do the driving =)*

> *7:37 p.m.* **Paul**: *Sorry I just saw your text! Hate to ask you to drive again, but I already started watching a movie. Can you come over here again?*

- Lack of spontaneous conversation (you cannot engage in the give-and-take that's necessary for open, honest exchanges when they are controlling the rate and flow of their outgoing messages, which you're impatiently waiting for with growing frustration) As stated above, they control the time elapsed between communications and it becomes easy for them to "forget" to respond to one of your earlier questions. You're always at the mercy of *their* desired timetable for resuming the conversation. You will communicate with them when *they* want, and *only* when they want. The conversation becomes stilted and stalled, with herky-jerky snippets that never result in a smooth flow of open communication. They are controlling your ability to have a constructive dialogue with them without appearing overtly aggressive and controlling. The absence of spontaneous conversation allows for details to get lost in the time lapse. Entire sentences can be ignored, and questions routinely go answered. The passive aggressive phone texter has perfected the art of the "accidental" blow-off with their delayed response time-management system.

> *10:01 a.m.* **Joe:** *My car is in the shop. Can you pick me up after work tonight? I'm off at 5 but could leave earlier since I know you get off at 4*

> *3:54 p.m.* **Joe's fiancée:** *What happened to your car?*

> *3:55 p.m.* **Joe:** *It stalled on my way to work and I had to get it towed. I can stay here until 7 if you're busy now, but the office gets locked up after that. Also, could you give me a ride to work tomorrow? A co-worker said they can drop me off at the station at lunch time when the car is supposed to be ready*

> *7:49 p.m.* **Joe's fiancée:** *Just saw your response. Do you still need a ride?*

- Cryptic ambiguous words can be carefully chosen, given the amount of time afforded by the above mentioned time delays. It takes a lot of thought and planning to cultivate creatively deceptive responses! Here's one of my all-times favorites from a man who was deceiving me from a thousand miles away. We'd been conversing on a nightly basis and suddenly he went AWOL:

> *Friday 7:30 p.m.* **Me:** *Hey, how was your day? Tried to call*

> *Saturday 8:15 p.m.* **Me:** *Left you a message. Miss you! Call when you're free*

And like any passive aggressive enabler, I suddenly turned into the protector. I became worried about his sudden withdrawal, and left several messages inquiring about his welfare. Finally, I received a response.

> *Sunday: 3:46 p.m.* **Guy:** *I'm fine*

The light bulb finally clicked on in my head.

> *Sunday: 3:47 p.m.* **Me:** *Sorry for the repeated interruptions. I'm a little dense. It just dawned on me that you've got someone else with you*

> *Sunday 4:17 p.m.* **Guy:** *I knew you would think that*

Greatest ambiguous response ever! *He knew I would think that? Probably because....it was true.* But he deliberately chose words that would mislead me into believing he was *not* with another woman. He must have been congratulating himself for being so clever. Yes, in fact, he later confessed that he did have a steady girlfriend the entire time he was stringing me along from afar.

When you choose to deceive by misleading someone with ambiguous words, you're kidding yourself if you don't call it a lie. In fact it's worse than lying, because you're intentionally causing someone to believe an untruth, and then you're patting yourself on the back for *not* lying. When you tell a bald face lie, at least you feel the shame of it as it's coming out of your mouth. That guy must have been priding himself for being so deceptively truthful. Or truthfully misleading? Between his deceptive words and his "hidden" life on Facebook, he surely made a fool out of me.

When we realize we've been deceived by ambiguities, it hurts our pride the most because our intelligence has been outwitted. We were outsmarted by someone we trusted to be straight with us, and we naively believed the distortion they so aptly gave us of the truth. We're frustrated and angry with ourselves for being so quick to believe the *impression* the words gave us, instead of immediately realizing the words were unclear. Passive aggressive people seem to have perfected the art of answering questions without giving straight answers. Some of them are so quick;

they don't even need the time delay of texting to think them up.

My favorite passive aggressive ex-boyfriend, Chris, is one of those people. He is, perhaps, the funniest guy I know. His wit rivals any stand-up comic, and his intelligence is off the charts. Oh yeah, and he's very handsome too. It's a lethal combination when you're a woman with a penchant for funny, intelligent, handsome men. Throw in the passive aggression and Chris was my finest strain of crack cocaine. I was addicted to his humor and charm, and when he evaded my questions and eluded my attempts to make plans with him, I was laughing too hard to get mad at him. He is the charming version of passive aggression.

A Friday night phone call with Chris:

> *Me: I'm finally gonna get a weekend off. If I fly to see you in California next weekend, can you meet me in San Diego?*

> *Chris: I'm not sure. I may have to work*

Coming from a man who hasn't worked a Saturday since he was 17

> *Me: When will you know your "schedule"?*

> *Chris: I should know by Sunday*

> *Me: Well you gotta let me know by Sunday morning before the flights go up*

> **Chris**: *Ok, I'll get back to you by Sunday night*
>
> **Me**: *Morning. Sunday morning*
>
> **Chris**: *Sunday morning. Got it*

Monday evening:

> **Chris**: *Hey, did you book that flight yesterday? I checked 'em today and they went up $400!*

Duh. It's Monday Dickhead. No, I didn't book the flight because you never called me back on Sunday.

While I can now laugh about all the times I've been eluded by men who started hedging when they felt like a woman was trying to exert control over them, it was frustrating for me when I was trying to forge closer relationships with these men.

The passive aggressive tactics that are routinely used by the offenders on Facebook do not usually fall into the extreme version of this behavior that disrupts relationships between couples and families. But it's hurtful, just the same.

The harsh reality is that you cannot change the behavior of others. You can only change the way you respond to it. That seems elementary, and yet there are grown men and women who believe they can change their partner's behavior. I, too, thought with time, patience, love, and understanding, I could alter the way a passive aggressive man responded to my normal expectations. It didn't occur to me that the men were quite happy being the way they were. It also didn't dawn on me that their passive aggressive behavior was one of their main attractants for me. I was addicted to feeling like I had to work for a man's attention. I prodded for his attention, and he pushed back. I went overboard trying to be the "good girlfriend" and he responded by cancelling out on plans at the last minute. I cooked elaborate meals and he didn't show up. He told me he had to go to a meeting after work and then later filled me in on the lively discussion he had with his co-worker's girlfriend at the bar they were all partying at. I was never invited to accompany him to functions where others regularly brought their dates. I gave him foot rubs and refilled his drink so he never had to leave the couch. He thanked me for being so nice and then pointed out how beautiful an actress was on the television. I was silently but aggressively shown that I was not good enough and not going to be included in his life unless he wanted me on *his* time, his terms. I felt continually hurt in small ways, and my own self-esteem was ratcheting down, one blow-off at a time.

> **Chris**: *Aren't we supposed to meet in San Diego this weekend?*

> **Me**: *Very funny*

> **Chris**: *No seriously, we gotta get together soon. I'll have to check my schedule. I'm playin' golf with my brothers one weekend*

I got angrier and angrier at the men, until I finally realized it was me that I should be angry with. These men were not doing anything to me that I wasn't *allowing* them to do. I was laying myself out there as a doormat, and then acting so shocked when I got stepped on. I owned my own hurt feelings, and I was responsible for allowing myself to be treated as "less-than." So I stopped blaming the men and started asking myself why I accepted this treatment.

> ***Chris****: Where did you go? You never call. You don't write. I have no way to get ahold of you. I've been worried sick!*
>
> ***Me****: Ha. Ha. I left you three messages this weekend*
>
> ***Chris****: No seriously. When are we gettin' together?*
>
> ***Me****: The only weekend I'm off is in two weeks*
>
> ***Chris****: You're kiddin! That's the weekend I'm playin' golf!*
>
> ***Me****: I could never pre-empt a golf game. So you're playing golf for three days straight?*

My parents used to get frustrated with me because I didn't stick up for myself whenever I got teased. I seemed to have been born with an inability to assert myself and defend my own honor. I just wimped out and started crying if my older sister teased me. And now I was a grown woman, doing the same thing. I was obviously attracted to men who aggravated my self-worth issues. I was in my 40's and I was still just wimping out, pointing the finger of blame at the one who teased my low self-worth. So I hibernated for a while and worked on my own issues. I cooked *myself* elaborate meals. I lit candles to give myself ambience. When I noticed the calendar was turning over to an ex-boyfriend's birthday, I bought myself a pedicure instead of a birthday present for an unappreciative man. Even if I was exhausted, I made myself do something that made *me* feel good. If I had no energy to do anything except crash into bed, I forced myself to dig out a pretty silky nightgown that had previously been reserved for special nights with a man. I started putting myself first without feeling guilty for spoiling myself. *I* appreciated the spoiling, while the men had not. My nurturing did not go unnoticed by *me*. And after I felt thoroughly pampered every evening, I sat down with a cup of coffee or a glass of wine and began plumbing the depths of my own psyche. Night after night, I would sit on the couch absent-mindedly staring into space, trying to figure myself out. Why was I attracted to people who hurt me by injuring my self-worth? Instead of stewing over past injuries that had been inflicted by people who showed complete disregard for my feelings, I put myself in their shoes and asked, why not? Why not take advantage of someone who clearly wants to be taken for granted? Why not allow a nurturing woman with no expectations to nurture you? Why not let someone stroke your ego when they're not demanding equal ego-stroking in return? It wasn't *their* problem. What was wrong with me?

> ***Chris****: Hey I was thinking we could stay one night in the Gaslamp Quarter when you're here*
>
> ***Me****: I didn't book the ticket. You never got back to me*
>
> ***Chris****: Damn. I was out of cell phone range*
>
> ***Me****: In your house*
>
> ***Chris****: Well there's only like four square feet in my house where I get coverage. You know how I pace around. It's not even worth dialing*
>
> ***Me****: In a forty-eight hundred square foot house there's only four feet of cell phone coverage. You've got a fifty-four hundred dollar a month mortgage.... but you can't swing the eight dollars a month for a landline*

I spent months in my reclusive self-reflective period. Friends started wondering if I was ever going to come up for air. While I appeared to be anti-social and disinterested in life, I was actually doing the most important internal work I had ever undertaken: figuring myself out.

I began scarfing up every self-help book I could find. I reached out to my friends in the metaphysical community, and began having daily conversations with one of my best friends, spiritual advisor Terryee

Abbott. Terryee helped me write my own mantra for self-love. I began reciting my mantra every day.

I was on a mission to get to the bottom of my issues and resurrect myself. I typed a question into a search engine on my computer. "Why am I a doormat?" It pulled up a book written by Lynne Namka, Ed. D, entitled, **The Doormat Syndrome**. The words on Dr. Namka's website jumped out at me. There was brief description about passive aggression. I was stunned. It was as if she had taken a page right out of my life in the description of passive aggressive men and the women who love them. She was not only describing the man's behavior to a tee, but she was describing me with exacting precision. I finally had an answer to what was wrong with me. I was addicted to passive aggression. I was tormented by it; I hated it, but I couldn't get enough of it. Why?

I resumed my journey into myself. Why did I have this issue?

> **Chris**: *You get a flight?*

> **Me**: *Seriously? I'm tired of trying to make plans with you. MY schedule doesn't allow me to change last-minute when YOU decide what YOU want to do*

> **Chris**: *What do you mean? I already booked us a room at the Sheraton overlooking the bay*

Putting social media and cell phones aside for a moment, let's look within *you*.

While I agree with Sigmund Freud on the point that many of our issues come from our relationships with parents, I firmly believe that our parents were chosen for us because they would cause us to work on issues we were already being born into this world with. Whether you believe in repeating lives, or reincarnation, doesn't matter. You can probably remember having fears when you were a child that you now view as completely unfounded. You wonder why you had those fears because your parents were not abusive. I remember being afraid that my parents were going to die. I was deathly afraid of being orphaned. I have no idea how I got that idea into my head. I did not know any orphans, nor had I ever heard of children without parents when I first began worrying about that. Can I blame my parents for my fear of being abandoned? No. It seems to me I was just "born" with that fear of losing someone who was crucial to my existence. Was it a pre-life premonition or pre-birth knowledge of the loss I was to experience later in life; losing my son? I have my own ideas about that, but this is not a debate about predetermined life agreements.

My point is, no matter how kind, loving, stable, secure, and non-judgmental our parents are, many of us seem to have come into this world with irrational fears. We can't blame everything on our parents. Not only do we have unfounded fears to contend with, but we also seem to have a predisposition to gravitate towards certain types of people. And yes, often they are people who remind us of our parents in some way.

You may have married a controlling woman, and although her personality is quite different from your mother, the controlling behavior may be a common thread between your wife and your mother. Your spouse does not always represent qualities in your parent of the same sex, though. Maybe your father was the control freak. Regardless of which parent your spouse seems to channel on some level – whether it's a pleasing or an irritating level, you very often do "marry your parent."

The reason we do this is because, as the shrinks often say, we are healing our inner child. We are drawn to people who will aggravate those old wounds (whether from childhood or earlier.) We're basically breaking open those old psychological wounds so that we will be able to go back and heal them as an adult. As children, we did not possess the emotional maturity to heal them ourselves. So the wounds have been lying dormant for years – maybe decades, and usually have years of scar tissue built up around them. We essentially have to rip off the layers of scar tissue, re-open the wound, and apply our adult's emotional maturity and wisdom to finally heal the wound.

If you look at the most painful or negative feelings you've had in current relationships, those same feelings almost always have much deeper roots that started growing in earlier relationships. Of course the situations are always different. But the old feelings are the same. Feelings of inadequacy or powerlessness or unworthiness get echoed repeatedly within different relationships until we finally heal those gaping wounds in our self-worth. Problematic behavior in others that previously caused you pain will reassert itself in future partners until you resolve your own issues surrounding that behavior. We call this love/hate attraction.

The thing we hate the most about our partners is often the greatest attractant, believe it or not. It's not that we love the behavior that causes those negative feelings inside us, but rather we need to work through our own issues surrounding that behavior in order to release our negativity. So in reality, that problematic behavior is exactly what we're drawn to. It's like the old adage of always wanting "the challenge." We chase the romantic prospects who present a challenge to our ego in the timeless pursuit of "winning" their hearts in order to inflate our own egos. While you may hate the fact that the challenging person makes you feel insignificant or unworthy, the fact that they illicit feelings of unworthiness inside of you is exactly what makes you so attracted to them. You want to feel worthy; therefore, you want that person to deem you worthy of their affection and you work very hard to prove yourself worthy. And therein lays the problem. You cannot get your own self-worth from another person. We've all seen the effects of that futile attempt. If you're looking for someone else to give you your own self-esteem, invariably that person will reject you at some point, and then you'll be left wallowing with lower self-esteem than you started with.

The funny thing about love/hate attraction is that it always feels like real love, but it's not. The feelings of attraction are very intense when someone aggravates a deep wound that you need to heal. It's almost like fatal attraction. You can become obsessed with thoughts of winning their affection, because the child inside of you believes that will stop the old wounds from hemorrhaging. It doesn't. The bleeding won't stop until you recognize the issues that person is causing you to work on, and resolve those issues within yourself. The even funnier thing about love/hate attraction is that when you finally resolve your own internal issues with the behavior that you hate, you suddenly "fall out of love" with that person. You were actually never *in* love with them, but just addicted to the feelings they cause you to surface. You need to work through those feelings and that person acts as a saddle burr, prodding you on. When you finally work through the negative feelings, the relationship has served its purpose. The relationship no longer serves you, and your feelings change. You begin viewing that person with clarity, in the light of truth. You see them for whom and what they really are, instead of the illusion of perfection your mind created to keep you in that relationship, working through your issues. Basically, your mind has been playing a trick on you, pulling you into a relationship that will force you to confront your own negative feelings that certain behaviors in others illicit. Your mind has been citing all these great qualities about that person, to encourage your desire to maintain that relationship. But when you finally conquer your own demons, the attraction diminishes and you realize you never had *real* love for that person. Sometimes, you can't figure out what attracted you to them in the first place, and years later you're asking the question, "Why did I waste so much time with them? I don't even *like* them!"

This brings me back to my own issues with passive aggression, which probably mirror some of yours. I hate this behavior, and yet historically I've quite obviously been drawn to men who exhibit it. It's a behavior which always made me feel unworthy, insignificant, manipulated, and taken advantage of. It made me feel "less-than." As with other passive aggressive enablers, I always put my own needs and desires on the back burner to be the "fixer." From outward appearances, I had no needs. Nope, not me. It was all about the man. How could I make *his* life better? I would tippy-toe around when he was in a quietly angry mood, trying not to bother him, taking care of everything by myself as every good fixer will do. I would never take him to task when he hurt me, no matter how deeply or how severely he overstepped normal boundaries. When he routinely cancelled plans, blew me off, ignored me, forgot me, or hurt me with words, I rarely even raised an objection. After all, it was all about him and *his* feelings.

> *Chris: You're lookin' a little bedraggled there*

> *Me: I'm just wiped out. Had to get up at three to catch the red eye. You about ready to go back to the room?*

> **Chris**: *Yeah, I'm just gonna play one quick game of pool with these guys. I'll get you a drink*
>
> **Me**: *Thanks. Then I'll only have to stay awake for twenty-five hours straight instead of twenty-three*

Let me point out, it takes two to maintain an unhealthy relationship. The man was no more to blame than I was. Had I forced him to confront the pain he caused me and demanded different dynamics by changing my own behavior, I assure you that change would have occurred or I would have left the relationship. But the enabler never forces the issue, which is the equivalent of fostering the unhealthy behavior. I'm sure I complained at times, but never too loudly. I might have threatened to walk away, but never followed through with my threats in a non-emotional resolute manner. With passive aggressive people, you must draw the line in the sand and stand your ground. If you allow them to treat your feelings with disregard without suffering consequences, you're just promoting their hurtful behavior and it will surely continue.

> **Me**: *Do you want to go into the Christmas shop?*
>
> **Chris**: *Is that a trick question?*
>
> **Me**: *Well, I want to go in that shop. Do you mind?*

> *Chris: I'll just wait outside and make a few phone calls. I need to call that girl from work back*
>
> *Me: I guess the two hours you spent talking to her when we were having breakfast didn't resolve her issues. Let's go to that cool clothing store after this*
>
> *Chris: Yeah she asked me to get her a souvenir sweat shirt. You can help me pick one out for her*

The more mixed signals I got from a man, the more I desperately tried to hang onto him. Although I knew I was supposed to read his behavior instead of his words, I wanted to believe his empty words. If the man said he loved me, I wanted to believe that. But his behavior showed me differently. I would never treat someone I love the way I was treated by several men. I can't blame the men, though. I *allowed* myself to be mistreated. With a couple of men, I think I was almost begging for it.

After numerous painful relationships with passive aggressive men, I finally drew that line in the sand. I realized it was *my* issue with passive aggression, and I worked hard to conquer my addiction to being treated with disregard. I found my self-worth and my self-worth was coming out with a vengeance, throwing wild punches in every direction that threatened it. In fact, I threw one too many punches and threw away a perfectly wonderful man whose only transgression was to say something that reminded me of a passive aggressive ex. Hey, I never said I was perfect. Sometimes we overcompensate when we're healing from a breakup and we're firmly entrenched in the self-protection mode. Shit happens, we make mistakes, but I always try to learn from them.

>*Me: Now you call me?*

>*Chris: What's wrong? I was playing golf*

>*Me: I'm done. I can't do this anymore*

>*Chris: What? What did I do now?*

>*Me: You haven't returned my calls for five days*

>*Chris: But I was playing golf with my brothers*

>*Me: For five entire days and nights. You didn't have five minutes to make a quick phone call to me*

>*Chris: But we were playing golf at Torrey Pines*

>*Me: I'm sure your brothers found five minutes to call their wives at some point*

>*Chris: Yeah. But they didn't **want** to*

And miracles happen. I finally cured myself of my addiction to passive aggression. I'm not saying I still don't feel the instinctive urge to pursue a man who isn't putting as much energy into our relationship as I am at times. I'm simply saying I have learned to run in the other direction when my intuition detects the tiny red flags I've come to know so well, because they've hurt me so deeply. I understand the difference between open-hearted men who are juggling busy lives, and their passive aggressive counterparts who control our relationship with low-level hostility which I do not deserve. I will never again be a bottom-feeder in someone's pond, settling for scraps of attention and crumbs of affection that rarely make it down to me. I stopped looking at the man accusingly and wondering why he treats me like I'm not worth his time, and started asking myself, "Am I not worth more than this...to *me*?"

How do you end your addiction to hurtful behavior? You begin by identifying the behavior that you're obviously drawn to and make a conscious decision to change the way you react to that behavior.

Think back to the rat experiment in psychology class. If the rat gets positive reinforcement, it will continue repeating the behavior that brought the reinforcement. They say that repeating the same behavior and expecting different results is the definition of insanity. If that were true, we'd all be insane. We humans appear to be slower learners than the rats are. We repeat the same behaviors with different partners, hoping for a different outcome. We're essentially repeating the same failed relationship over and over with different people.

While we can't change the way others behave, we can change the way we react to their behavior. And while we still may feel hurt by that behavior in others, knowledge is power. Recognizing the hurtful behavior, putting a name on it, and consciously choosing to refrain from letting it affect our lives enables us to change our habitual reactions.

Just as I was addicted to passive aggressive behavior in different men, you can become addicted to one person in particular who delivers your form of heroin. When you're addicted to a person, you're always looking at them through a rosy lens. You make excuses for their behavior and justify it in your mind. If they ignore you, you tell yourself their schedule is just so busy they don't have time for *anyone*, but you're certain they'd really love to see you if they could. You convince yourself they're grappling with so many headaches of their own that they couldn't possibly make time to address your feelings and your relationship. But you believe eventually they will suddenly find the time. You think they've been jaded by other partners who just didn't understand them like you do, and you keep hanging on believing you will be the one who finally teaches them how to love.

If you struggle with an unhealthy addiction to a relationship, I'd recommend, **How to Break Your Addiction to a Person**, by Howard Halpern.

When someone is important to you, you always make time for them. The person you love is the one whose calls you always answer. The same applies for someone who loves *you*. They're never too busy to make time for you. They address your feelings and make visible attempts to show you they care. They show their love for you in a thousand tiny ways, instead of showing you red flags of rejection amidst a million tiny acts of inconsideration.

A Look Behind the Offender's Offenses

Let's begin by admitting we are *all* offenders. We've all done some of these things – or all of these things – to a greater or lesser degree. So keep in mind when we're labeling folks "offenders," that label applies to all of us. The ability to laugh at ourselves is inherent to our self-acceptance and self-love. You won't learn anything by pointing fingers and calling names, unless you're doing this in front of a mirror.

But instead of name calling, let's just pose a question instead: Why? Why do we engage in behavior that is transparently immature or dysfunctional, and frequently harmful to our relationships?

Reason #1: We want attention.

Reason #2: We want vindication.

Reason #3: We want flattery.

Reason #4: We want revenge.

Reason #5: We want drama.

Reason #6: We want control.

Most of the Facebook foibles would fall into Reason #1; craving attention. That's not really a bad thing. We all crave interaction with other human beings. But if we're struggling with low self-worth, we crave attention even more. In fact, we'd like to be the *center* of attention when we're full of self-doubt and our ego has left the building.

Consider the average worker. Most of us are subordinate to someone, but regardless of how many bosses we may or may not have, we all feel overworked and under-appreciated. We get work piled on our desk which we never seem to reach the bottom of. We get swamped at the office with unreasonable deadlines, no time for coffee breaks, and no thank you's. We work with cranky, competitive co-workers who never acknowledge our efforts. We work with the public, which by-and-large is angry and impatient with us. We stock the shelves in retail stores which never close. Our customers and clients look right through us without seeing a person. They see a cashier who won't give them a discount, or a reservations clerk who can't get that plane to land any faster. They speak to a customer service representative who can't reconfigure their computer settings over the phone.

Consider stay-at-home-moms-and-dads. We spend hours cooking, cleaning, nurturing, loving, refereeing, chauffeuring, tutoring, doctoring, and worrying about everyone else's welfare. But no one ever asks how *we're* doing.

We feel invisible all day, every day. We feel overlooked and overwhelmed. And boring. We don't feel unique and special to anyone.

But we can sign online after everyone else goes to bed and suddenly we're the star. We're commended for our amusing remarks. Our humor and sensitivity are actually noted and appreciated. People converse with us, instead of talking *at* us and seeing through us. Behind our computer screen, we're no longer invisible. So attention-getting is not such a bad thing. It's just annoying when some of our friends take the art of grabbing attention to new heights.

But consider how overlooked and insignificant those friends must feel in order to beg for attention so often. Their good days must be worse than your worst months. They feel utterly miserably invisible, and so they must constantly put themselves in front of you, begging for attention. They're like a little kid jumping up and down, "Look at me! Look at me!" Their own inner child is that same little kid who goes to bed sadly wondering why the other kids get all the attention. Yeah, it may be irritating behavior in an adult. But we're not dealing with adult behavior when we're dealing with Facebook foibles.

Next comes Reason #2: Vindication. It's human nature to desire vindication when we feel we've been wronged. Not only do we want to feel justified, but we feel the support of others is necessary to prove ourselves right. We want sounding boards. We want to explain our side of the story to impartial observers and be cited as the one who is right. We want a jury to find us "not guilty." Our network of friends conveniently serves as the jury. So we post "our side of the story" in our own words, in the words of others through songs or inspirational quotes, or in pictures which tell their own story.

Social media is a convenient way of telling our side of the story without having to confront the other side. The other guy won't get equal time if they're not part of our friend network. If they are, then we can engage in a non-verbal battle, attacking each other through postings. No confrontation necessary. Just read-between-the-lines-and-you'll-see-who-is-right vindication. This is the child begging for its mother to scold the older sibling for teasing or otherwise "being mean." We want someone to stick up for us. The more people we enlist on our side, the better the vindication. Preferably the whole kindergarten class.

Flattery is Reason #3, and it's similar to the first reason, yet different. Flattery isn't simply getting attention, but getting praise and admiration. This is the ego wanting to be stroked. When the first child says, "Look at me!" the second child says, "No, look at me! Isn't my cartwheel the best?" We all want our cartwheels to be admired. We want the ego boost that flattery delivers, and solicit admiration in feeble attempts at making ourselves feel better about ourselves. We assume we'll have more self-esteem if others envy or admire us. We assume wrong.

When my daughter was growing up I used to tell her, "Don't ever look to the boys to give you your self-esteem. You can only get that from yourself." Susie was in middle school when I began drilling this into her head. I think by the time she hit 9th grade, she had a firmer grasp on that concept than many adults do. But many adults didn't have someone encouraging them to foster their own self-worth during their formative years, so we're on Facebook posting cartwheel pictures for our middle-aged friends to gawk at. Yes, your boat's bigger than mine. Oh wait, I don't have a boat. You win.

Reason #4: Revenge! We've all been hurt and it's instinctive for us humans to want paybacks. We need The Inspirational Quoting Hatchet Murderer to remind us that "To err is human; to forgive divine." Vengefulness has the same simmering acidic quality that jealousy does. In fact, the two often go hand in hand in broken romances. Jealousy eats you up from the inside out, and then the desire for revenge slithers into the pool of bitter bile. People who have been abandoned by their romantic partner may mourn their loss for a bit, and then suddenly become vengeful. They want their ex to pay for hurting them. This seems to be the most common form of revenge that's played out on the Facebook walls of ex-lovers everywhere. It comes in the form of slanderous posts, unfriending, hatchet wielding inspirational quotes, and pictures from self-promoters intent on making themselves appear happier without their ex. People seem to put a lot of thought and energy into elaborate vengeful tactics, which only makes them dwell on their unhappiness more. "Happiness is the best revenge," is the best quote to live by. Revenge turns us into very small miserable people. Forgiveness frees us to move on to greener pastures with happy endings "in a relationship."

Reason #5: Drama: The drama diva could not come up with a better invention. Social media allows you to stir up drama at any time, any place, at your convenience. The drama lovers can wreak havoc in the lives of others without ever leaving their own homes. They don't need to put on make-up to flirt with your man. They don't need to flirt with your girlfriend to post something that raises suspicious eyebrows. And the beauty of social media platforms is that everyone can participate! Even if you don't normally cause drama yourself, you can live vicariously through the misfortunes of others who got caught in the gossip chain. It's like voyeurism, watching the drama unfold between friends. Better than a soap opera. If there's nothing good to watch on television, just sign online and you'll have all the drama you can stand.

Like many passive aggressive enablers, I truly loathe drama, which is the reason why I historically let the hurtful behavior go unchecked. I didn't want to fuss and fight over my own hurt feelings, so I didn't put them on the table for discussion. I just glossed things over and swept unacceptable behavior under the rug, trying to be the peacekeeper with no feelings of my own to be concerned with. But I have discovered that many people who claim to hate drama are actually drawn to it, if not being the instigators of it. It's that love/hate attraction thing again. Men are typically the ones who say they hate drama, and yet all the passive aggressive men I've dated are the underlying source of all the drama in their lives, which has occasionally muddied *my* life. Secrets, lies, betrayals and lover's triangles have been uncovered via Facebook, while I was never confronted in person by a man's desire to end our relationship. I had to discover his true intentions through his Facebook activity, which in turn stirred up gossip in *my* life when friends noticed his changes in relationship status, the elimination of pictures, etc. I seemed to be the last to know my boyfriend had strayed. And as a drama-hater myself, I was forced to deal with betrayal while trying to actually cover up for the cheating man, because I didn't want any *more* drama. I wanted to lick my wounds in private, but his Facebook activity didn't allow me to sidestep his public withdrawal from our relationship. While he was claiming to "hide" me in order to keep his private life private, he was making our issues very public. I was the one who was desperately trying to maintain a sense of privacy by keeping our dirty laundry out of the public forum, while he was essentially broadcasting it to everyone without verbalizing it to me.

This seems to be a common scenario on Facebook, even if the person doesn't exhibit other forms of passive aggression. It's a spineless way to avoid addressing issues while making your point. It's the chicken-shit way out. And it's dramatic.

But why do we secretly love drama? Because we're bored. We're the little kid who doesn't know what else to do and our favorite Gilligan's Island show got pre-empted by a political debate, so we pick on our younger brother to stir something up. He cries and we may get in trouble, but we broke the boredom; our main concern. Drama brings excitement into the doldrums of our daily lives. While we may appear to be the non-descript account executive, teacher, mom, librarian, we can live vicariously through the drama unfolding on Facebook. We can even be a part of it by simply commenting on someone else's drama. It enlivens our boring lives and gives us something to gossip about with our friends... all the while saying, "I hate drama!"

And here's the biggie: Reason #6: We want CONTROL. We all like to feel that we're in control of our own lives, and the biggest irritant with social media is the lack of control we have over other's postings. We've carefully chosen photos to represent us, funny sayings and pictures to let the world know we've got a sense of humor, we've "liked" our favorite singers, books, stores, movies, and actors in an effort to give others a representation of our personality and character. And then someone else posts something that we feel may cast us in an unflattering light, and we immediately get our bristles up, ready to do Facebook battle. Our Twitter artillery is at the ready, and our personal web pages are primed and ready to deflect criticism with our own stockpile of poison arrows.

How dare they post that about me? How dare they flaunt something that caused me pain? We abhor the amount of control social media gives others over personal aspects of our lives, and yet we're addicted to it.

Facebook seems to be the first thing on people's minds when they have a life altering experience. People get married and before they hit the honeymoon suite, they change their status to "married." My daughter took a lot of guff for "not knowing the day she got married" because a Facebook posting wasn't the first thing on her mind on her wedding day, July the 7th. When she changed her relationship status days later, it said, "Susie got married on July 11th!" I was happy she was enjoying her honeymoon instead of worrying about status changes on Facebook.

I've known several people who were so devastated after a break-up; I became worried when they sounded suicidal in their tearful phone calls to me directly after the break-up. But minutes after they had been dumped, their status changed. Is that really the first thing on your mind when you feel you can't live another moment on earth? *Let me change my status to "single" before I slit my wrists.*

It's all about control. The heartbroken lovers wanted to be the one who controlled their relationship status and publicized that news first themselves. It's the typical image problem we all struggle with. We're worried about what others think of us more than we're worried about what we think of ourselves. We're back in grade school, feeling the sting of being a victim of secret-telling. So we hurry and pass a note around about the secret tellers themselves. We want control over our situation and reputation, and we'll act now and think later. The wrist slitting contemplation can wait until we've made our side of the story public.

And here is where the clinically described "passive aggressive" person connects with Facebook. Control. Passive aggression is defined by Lynne Namka, Ed. D, as: "A dynamic born of fear of being controlled, fear of confrontation, hidden anger and an inability to deal straight with people."[1]

Passive aggressive people fight back if they believe someone else is trying to control them. But they use their own passive means of getting what they want, without verbally confronting someone in person. Often times, the passive aggressive man is the "nice guy" who appears genuinely sweet and easy-going. He verbally agrees to compromising and showing up when he's expected. But when it comes down to his actions, he will do whatever he pleases. He's continually resisting his partner through non-verbal means, which draws frustration and anger out in his partner. It's almost like he's goading her into expressing the anger that he feels but cannot express himself. He needs her, but he pushes her away. He isn't ready to commit, but he wants that woman in his corner. He wants her attention and concern, but he feels entitled to his own freedom. He holds the ultimate control over the relationship's progression, and always keeps people at a distance by withdrawing, resisting, and rebelling in small ways. He's very self-protective and he may have multiple relationships with different women, so none of them can get too close to him. He may be torn between women and can't make a decision, and his behavior effectively sandbags both of them.

Social media is a convenient way to appear available to friends, while not really being available to the people who are close to you. You can post without having a discussion with someone. You can keep your wall hidden so that no one can post anything without your permission. You can keep secrets while appearing to be open and reachable. You can hide your friends list and make status bars visible to selected people. You can maintain control!

Facebook: The Greatest Passive Aggressive Weapon EVER

Relationships: To Hide or Not to Hide

Single, in a relationship, or nobody's business? This is a big topic of debate amongst Facebook users. People seem to fall clearly on one side of the argument or the other. The easiest way around the argument is to simply hide the relationship status column, which is my preference.

There are those who vehemently decry it as an invasion of privacy and they do not want their significant other to be linked to them via the "in a relationship with so-and-so" column. Yet if they leave their relationship status visible as "single" it hurts their partner's feelings.

There are others, like myself, who feel if the relationship has progressed to the point where I refer to the man as "my boyfriend," then he deserves the respect that a visible boundary represents if he would like it, and I will unhide my relationship status and check the "in a relationship" box. I certainly won't advertise myself as "single." I'm old-fashioned. When I see someone listed as "single," I assume they're unattached and playing the field. But to many folks, "single" simply means "not married." So even if they've been exclusively dating someone for years, they prefer to publicly display a "single" status in the relationship column.

While I don't believe that Facebook should define a relationship, I do believe that it's necessary to protect your important relationships by acknowledging boundaries, whether you're online, in person, at work, or at play. If your publicly visible "single" status bothers your partner, you need to have a conversation before it turns into a bone of contention between you. I agree that a public display of a "single" status shouldn't lead people to assume that you're unattached and available to date. It *shouldn't*. But it *does*. So let's be real.

But with that said, most of us do not determine our loyalty based on a box we checked on Facebook. Wearing a wedding ring does not make every married person loyal, and listing yourself as "single" does not make you a cheater.

If your partner has unfounded insecurities of their own, there is little you can do to make them feel better about themselves and more secure in the relationship. But if their insecurities are driven by *your* behavior, then hiding your relationship with them will only add to their suspicion and doubt.

It comes down to whether both parties feel comfortable or uncomfortable publicly linking themselves to each other, and unfortunately both parties don't always agree. There are those people who are socially shy or very private people, and they don't want anyone asking them about their personal life. They may feel embarrassed or awkward if someone inquires about the relationship, and it's easier for them to avoid that turf altogether. That's a valid reason for hiding.

Then there are those who jump the gun immediately after they begin dating someone, and they want connected publicly with that person. They're in short supply of their own self-esteem and they feel their image would be improved with the addition of the romantic connection. Their low self-worth doesn't allow them to believe they're good enough standing all on their own. They view a romantic partner as proof that they're worthy and desirable, and they wish to advertise it.   These are the folks who are usually desperate for approval. They're latching onto any connection with another person which will validate them as worthy individuals and elevate their self-esteem. This is the unhealthy reason for choosing *not* to hide a relationship, because the relationship isn't being touted as much as the person's self-worth issues.

How about the unhealthy reason for *hiding* relationships?

Back to our list of passive aggressive offenders, The Hider is probably the greatest source of broken hearts. I have had my own broken a couple of times when the painful truth was illuminated for me by Facebook. On one occasion, the man who proclaimed to love me had been tagged in photos with another woman on a night he had told me he was sick. I saw them before he could hide them or untag himself. Another rude awakening happened when I signed on to post a funny remark on my boyfriend's wall and discovered he had hidden every picture that contained me. When I called him on it, he told me he was just tired of everyone knowing about his private life. Really? Now why would that bother someone who was loyal to the person they'd been dating for over a year? I must have missed the paparazzi that had suddenly started hounding him. Who knew our old vacation photos would suddenly start causing such a stir? *Okay, that was the pot calling the kettle black. Sarcasm is low-level passive aggression!*

People regularly post pictures of themselves with their partners until they decide to cheat, and suddenly they're worried about an invasion of privacy. Do they realize they're invading *your* privacy when you unknowingly began sharing a lover? STD anyone? Anyone up for an STD?

If you're selfishly maintaining two different relationships, you're lying to both people so you don't have to make a choice. By choosing one, you must let go of the other.   You may have your own issues surrounding indecision, taking ownership, fear of commitment, or passive aggression yourself. You're exercising the adult version of having your cake and eating it too. Unfortunately, both people usually find out about the deception. No matter how hard The Hider tries to hide things, someone always knows something and the ugly truth will eventually come to light.

The old rule of thumb I always go by is: If you're in a relationship you need to keep a secret from other people, you should not be in that relationship. When you're lying and cheating on two different people, you don't deserve *either* relationship. That doesn't mean you're a bad person. It just means you need to grow up and start making decisions that are in everyone's best interest, and not just your own. You're guilty of indecision and even though you don't want to hurt anyone, you will. When you're keeping secret relationships for your own personal gratification, you will always hurt the ones you are trying hardest to protect from the truth. If you truly don't wish to cause anyone pain, then don't do anything that you will feel the need to hide. Stand in your own truth, and put your truth out there for everyone to see. Healthy relationships between two loving individuals should not need to be kept a secret.

Unless you're a movie star – and most of us aren't – the public will not try to interfere with your relationship and invade your privacy. The real reasons most of us hide relationships are one of the following:

- We feel guilt for being in that relationship
- We feel ashamed of that relationship
- We know it will hurt someone else
- We know it will be frowned upon by our family, friends, or employers
- We want to appear openly available to date others

I look at Facebook as a giant dinner party. If we've agreed to date each other exclusively, then introduce me at the dinner party as your girlfriend. Any adult with an ounce of decency would not bring their girlfriend or boyfriend to a party and then pretend they were solo. The Hiders always claim to be protecting their privacy. How about protecting the relationship instead? If you truly want your exclusive relationship to be shielded from the public circle of gossip, then you will put boundaries around that relationship by acknowledging that it's important to you. The only privacy The Hider is usually protecting is their ability to pursue other conquests without appearing to be an opportunistic philanderer. Healthy adult relationships have boundaries which both partners maintain. Publicly putting up those boundaries around your important relationships actually fosters more privacy between the two of you by keeping public speculation out of the mix. It also allays suspicion and doubt in your partner's mind, which is necessary for keeping insecurities at bay and maintaining trust. So unless you and your partner both agree that you'd rather not let anyone know you're dating, this topic needs to be discussed before one of you gets an unpleasant surprise either way. If you want to keep it a secret but your partner doesn't and you're active on Facebook, you better have a damn good reason for keeping them off your wall.

If you've been hurt by The Hider's dirty little secrets being revealed online, take heart. The truth will set you free from people who abuse your affection. While betrayal hurts, especially if it's public, it's better to be informed through black and white or Kodachrome than to be ignorant of your situation. Hiders always get uncovered at some point, but their tangled web always weaves more secrets and lies as they frantically try to cover their tracks with more lies. Be thankful you will no longer be the one who gets hurt. Lick your wounds, work on yourself, and refrain from stalking their Facebook pages in search of more sordid details. If you honestly think they're treating their current partners any better than they treated you, then you need to keep reading. Leopards don't change their spots even if they're spotted with another leopard on Facebook.

Facebook: The Greatest Passive Aggressive Weapon EVER

Addiction to Secrets, Secret Lives and Secret Keepers

Why do secrets draw us in like a giant magnet? Why are we attracted to people who appear mysterious, elusive, and secretive? Why do we bypass friends and lovers who live clean, open, honest lives, in favor of the murky waters that surround secretive people? Do we believe they're hiding a heart of gold underneath the muddy surface?

We chase the elusive people who appear hard to get and guarded, and our curiosity drives us to uncover the secretive details of their private lives. We want to be privy to the inner-workings of their personal relationships, motivations, desires, and emotions. We pry beneath the surface for information, we stalk them on the web, we entertain ourselves imagining how it feels to be part of their inner circle, and we fantasize about being the one person they will finally open up to. We want to be in on the secret. We want drama. Secrets create drama under the surface, and it makes the people who keep them appear more alluring.

Are these secretive people really that exciting? Or is the excitement strictly based on our own anxious desire to be deemed worthy of inclusion into the circle of secrets? It makes us feel like we are part of the movie.

Let's say you have a crush on someone who appears unavailable to you. You don't know them well because they seem to be very private, but they're very attractive or outwardly popular, and you believe they're unattainable. They are involved with someone else or married. They may be someone you went to high school with or an acquaintance from work. You connect on Facebook, Classmates, LinkedIn, or just through private email. You begin exchanging emails, and perhaps phone calls. They begin confiding in you. They're struggling with personal drama in their life with a partner or a soon-to-be-ex. They don't confide in many people, and you feel honored to be entrusted with their personal agenda. You become the trusted ear, the confidante, the chosen one who is privy to all their secrets. You carry on this private, secretive relationship with them as they're going through the angst of disentangling themselves from their current relationship. They share the difficulties they are having with their current partner, who doesn't want to let them go. From where you're standing, it looks like their partner is obviously still in love with them, or otherwise clinging onto them for other reasons. They complain about their partner and their partner's attempts to repair things. They appear to be "in demand" and you begin viewing yourself as the special one who is getting the time and attention that their partner is desperate to have. You become part of the drama, part of the secret. You begin seeing each other on the sly, and an intimate relationship develops as they are "trying" to leave their current partner.

They *may* finally free themselves. Let's assume they do. You've become very close and you're now free to openly date each other. Your ego is soaring to new heights with your new designation as the chosen one, the winner. You won the heart of the person who was previously out of your reach, unattainable, and in demand.

Now what? Well, there is always that chance that you will fall madly in love each other and live happily ever after. But the odds are against that, because the initial attraction you felt to this relationship was not actual love for the person. You were attracted by your ego's desire to be found worthier than an opponent. You were attracted to the rush of getting the one that seemed impossible to get. And you were attracted to drama. The murky secretive waters of their life pulled you in. There was excitement beneath the surface. You became one of their secrets. Are you going to be content in this relationship now? That depends on how addicted you are to the feeling of insecurity.

Most likely, you will never feel completely secure in this relationship, because you already know first-hand that this person has no qualms about soliciting a new partner online, and you also know how many more opportunities are now available for meeting people through the internet. There is always another sympathetic ear; another shoulder to cry on if they should become unhappy or bored with you. When you're dating someone who is cheating on their partner, you're dating a cheater. You get what you pay for when you buy into their justifications for cheating.

It's the same old story we've always heard about having an affair with a married person. You know they're capable of infidelity from the get-go. They cheated on their ex with you, so what makes you think they won't cheat on you with someone else? The invention of the internet made a lot of things easier, including cheating. Unhappily married people used to routinely have office affairs or secret trysts with their neighbors, but they didn't have this huge pool of potential lovers available online. At the end of the day, they went home to their spouse. They didn't have the option of trolling online for mates after their spouse went to bed. The internet has given us more options for behaving badly. It's a lazy way of making dishonorable choices without being seen.

But you swear you're in love with the person who just deceived their previous flame by entering into a relationship with you before the last embers had died. Ask yourself, do you really respect this person now? Do you admire their character? Do you believe they're trustworthy? Do *you* want a partner who has shown a huge lack of integrity in their personal life? If you decide to pursue a relationship with this person, you're saying several things about yourself:

I deserve a partner who lies and cheats on me.

I want an insecure person who can't let go of one partner until they've gotten another one lined up.

I'm happy to have my partner air our dirty laundry to other would-be suitors.

This isn't you? When you are looking with desire at someone else's partner, you are wishing to be in their shoes. Look closely at the shoes they're wearing. Before you dive into the muddy water surrounding the intriguing and "attached" object of your affection, just imagine yourself wearing the shoes of the betrayed. You're wise enough to know that you're only hearing one side of the story, and the other side is clearly being deceived. If you'll enjoy the treatment their current partner is experiencing, then you deserve to have that relationship. We all deserve joy in our life.

The whole point of this book is not to simply make fun of people who utilize the internet and cell phones to disrupt healthy communication. The underlying intention is to make you realize you deserve healthy relationships with real people, authentic conversations that are not scripted and predicted, true love from a live person instead of a screen name who "likes" your profile. It's about finding your self-worth by identifying those things that erode it, and becoming cognizant of the negative influence passive aggression has on your relationships and your view of yourself.

Take a look at your own history of dating. Do you have a pattern of overlapping one relationship with another? Were you already "in talks" with your current partner before you officially broke it off with the previous one? If so, you're insecure with yourself and you don't feel confident to stand on your own. You always feel the need to have a partner in your corner. You don't feel valuable unless you have someone else beside you, wanting you, stroking your ego. Essentially, you haven't discovered your own self-worth, so you look outside of yourself to get that from others.

If you're currently attached, look at your partner. Do they have that history of overlapping one love interest with another? Were they striking up a burgeoning relationship with you while they were still attached to another? In spite of what they may tell you, can you see their timeline of dating reflects a habit of rebounding with a replacement as soon as they end a relationship? Deep down, do you honestly believe they ended each relationship before they began pursuing the person they immediately hooked up with afterwards?

If you're involved with someone who doesn't want to be alone, you're dating someone who is insecure with themselves. If they have a history of leaving no space of time between each relationship, you can bet they won't leave you until they have another person waiting in the wings. In other words, they may be grooming their next partner at this very minute, and you are none the wiser. You won't be privy to their "secret" relationship until they give you the boot and you may see their new flame on their Facebook wall shortly thereafter

If you are attracted to people who are insecure, you probably have issues with insecurity yourself. Instead of accusing those people of lacking self-confidence, look at your own issues. You're attracted to those people for some reason. Discover the reason and work on resolving your own issues with insecurity or insecure people, so that you can avoid the attraction drawing you in next time.

There are other reasons for being attracted to relationships that must be kept a secret. Commitment phobic people are notorious for this. They will chase the person who clearly cannot be committed to them or publicly attached to them; the married person, their co-worker, their best friend's ex, their ex-girlfriend's sister, the person who lives in another country. They don't want someone who is actually available to form a committed relationship with them. They prefer someone who "can't be seen" out in public with them. They'd rather be perceived as "single" while they're enjoying the benefits of having a partner behind closed doors.

The issues may not go as deep as actually having a phobia. People who are described as "players" may also be attracted to clandestine lovers. They don't want anyone else in the playing field to think they're off-limits, so they gravitate towards romantic partners they can't have an open relationship with. They will always come up with a logical sounding reason why "nobody should know" about your relationship with them. There is always a reason for keeping it in the closet, under wraps, and on the down-low.

If you're involved with someone like this, you're already seeing red flags all over the playing field. You see how easily they lie to cover up *your* relationship with them, and your higher consciousness takes note of how easily the lies roll off their tongue. Your mind wants to believe they are telling *you* the truth, but your intuition is calling foul. Once again, don't point fingers of blame. Why are *you* attracted to someone who doesn't want to acknowledge their relationship with you? Why are you letting someone chip away at your own self-worth?

Am I Passive Aggressive?

We all use passive tactics to get what we want sometimes. We may agree to run an errand for our spouse and then conveniently "forget." It's not that we are trying to make them upset. It's just that we really didn't want to run the errand, and we assumed it could wait until tomorrow.

Sometimes we get angry at someone and we withdraw from them instead of verbalizing our anger. They know we're mad, but we're not allowing them to address it with us, so it cannot be resolved. They may not know *why* we're mad, and it's frustrating for them.

Often we use mild passive aggressive tactics because we don't want to rock the boat with someone by openly asserting ourselves. So we passively go along with them but we find a way to get out of it.

Text messages are fantastic for this! We have all employed the delayed response time-management system that passive aggressive people routinely use. You're lying if you say you haven't done this.

Consider this scenario. You and I are friends, and you'd like me to go to a movie with you tonight. I really like you and value your friendship, but I'm exhausted and the only thing I want to do is go home, put my jammies on, and curl up in front of a corny old movie.

You call me on the phone and ask, "Do you want to go to the movies with me tonight?"

I have several choices for response.

Choice #1: I can lie. I can say yes I want to go, even though I really don't want to. But I value your friendship and don't want to hurt your feelings by turning down the invitation. I also want to make sure that you will continue to extend future invitations which I will gladly accept when I'm not so damn tired. So I can grudgingly go, but I won't be happy about it. I'll be secretly angry at myself for not honoring my own desire to stay home for the evening, and not having the guts to just tell you the truth instead of feeling obligated to do something I don't want to do.

Choice #2: I can lie. I can tell you I'd love to go but I've already made plans. This will require a follow-up lie if you ask me what my plans are. I will be required to invent a phony engagement, and this may require many follow-up lies in the future if you ask me to elaborate on the phony engagement.

Choice #3: I can tell you the truth. I don't want to go. Rejecting an invitation from a valued friend can be awkward and uncomfortable for both parties. Telling you the truth also requires me to put energy into ensuring your feelings are not hurt. I will feel the need to extoll all the reasons that I'm too tired to go out, and offer reassurances that I really do enjoy hanging out with you. Telling the truth will require a lengthier conversation and I'm just flat too tired for conversing.

But if you send me this invitation via text message, you present me with Choice #4: Ignore the text and pretend I didn't see it until it was too late. Then I can politely reply to you after I've deemed it safely "too late" to go to the movies.

> *I just saw your text!* (Lie)

> *I wish you would have just called me* (Big Lie)

> *I would have loved to have gone to the movies with you tonight* (Bigger Lie)

> *I didn't have anything planned* (Grain of truth)

> *I ended up just sitting home by myself watching a corny old movie* (Truth)

Our conscience always feels better if we can follow up a lie with some truthful statements. The grains of truth act like a cushion for our guilt to fall back on.

But what did that do for you? In my efforts to stay home without hurting your feelings, I effectively hit the pause button on your evening. You're polite and you don't want to rescind an invitation after you've extended it. You don't want to make other plans or invite someone else until you hear back from me. You're afraid of looking like a pest if you follow up with repeated texts or phone calls asking if I got your message. So you wait. And wait. And the clock ticks down and the opportunity for you to invite someone else and still make it to the movie on time is passing you by. I'm leaving you in limbo. I basically stalled your plans for the evening without doing a thing. And I'm over here congratulating myself for being so cleverly polite. I wasn't polite at all. I didn't take your time, effort, or feelings into consideration. I was doing what I wanted to do and blowing you off without appearing to blow you off.

Have you recently made plans with someone that you have no intention of keeping? How do you plan to get out of that? Will you cancel the plans ahead of time with an honest explanation? Or will you wait until the last minute and gracefully sidestep the plans somehow?

While most of us do employ these mildly passive aggressive tactics at times, we do not actually have the underlying issues that go along with the clinical description of passive aggression that prohibits development of healthy relationships. If you believe that you or a loved one suffers from this type of passive aggression, I would recommend counseling for everyone involved. The passive aggressive person can't operate without someone who acts as the receiver. As my own behavior suggests, it always takes two to tango.

There are many wonderful books on the market which will explain this behavior, the frequent causes of it, as well as tips to managing it from both sides. I don't profess to be a psychologist or any sort of an expert on this behavior. I'm just an average American Facebook user who struggles with common issues of low self-worth.

My good friend, Terryee, is a very intuitive psychic. You don't have to believe in clairvoyance to appreciate someone with wisdom. Terryee explained to me that people come from one of two places; they either come to you from love, or they come to you from fear. Everything else stems from those.

All of our warm and fuzzy emotions and behaviors come from a place of love. All of our negativity; in both emotions and behavior, comes from fear. So we always have a choice. We can choose to act in love or *re*act in fear.

It's easy for us to see where the fear creeps into our relations with others. We're conditioned to be self-protective. That's where our ego comes in. Our ego is basically our mind's creation of our image, and it struggles to protect that image. But is it a real image or a false image of us? The term "false image" is redundant. An image is an optical reproduction of something or someone real. Do you want to be your own illusionary representation? Or do you want your image to mirror the real you?

Fear is not reflective of the real you. Love is real. F.E.A.R. stands for False Evidence Appearing Real. But we let our fear control our behavior much of the time, instead of being driven by love-based motivations. Forgiveness comes from love. Jealousy is driven by fear. Humility is love-based. One-upmanship is motivated by fear of being unworthy. Passive aggression stems from fear of being controlled. Honesty comes from love; we love and honor ourselves as well as others by giving them real information.

So ask yourself which place *you* are coming from when you start looking within yourself and asking questions like, *Am I passive aggressive? Am I selfish? Am I envious? Do I really think I'm better than another person I'm disassociating with? Why am I doing something that will cause another pain? Where are these feelings coming from? My parents? My childhood? My ex? Pre-birth? No clue?*

You may be as startled as I was to discover there is one thing in particular that has caused you endless pain in different circumstances throughout your life.

Post-traumatic stress can be caused by relationships as well as war atrocities. People who have been abused by parents, spouses, or others can usually identify where their issues are stemming from rather easily. But if your relationships are still being affected by the abuse of the abuser, the abuser is still winning. They still have control over your life. They control your view of yourself and others, and they control how you relate to people who care about you. This is another area I'm not qualified to offer advice in, but I do know the frustration of being in a relationship with someone who has suffered emotional abuse from a partner. There's little you can do to help them until they decide to get help for themselves. As much as you love them, you may reach a point where you have to look out for your own survival. If you desire a healthy relationship and your partner is not open to seeking counseling for their emotional scars that create dysfunction in your relationship, you may resign yourself to looking for a different partner.

Facebook: The Greatest Passive Aggressive Weapon EVER

Confessions from Chris

The passive aggressive behavior that we all use on Facebook or text messaging is actually the "normal" mild version of this behavior. The men I've dated exhibited it to a much more extreme degree. I asked Chris to share his favorite avoidance tactics. He would have never been able to have this conversation with me if we were still dating. He's not only passive aggressive but he also shies away from commitment, which often goes hand-in-hand.

"So tell me Chris, what is it that makes you pull away from women you're dating? When they say passive aggression is a fear of control, does it actually feel like fear?"

"No, it's not like you're scared. It's like that feeling when you look at that name coming up on the cell phone and you say Aw shit. I don't want to have a *real* conversation. This person's going to want to have a *real* conversation. Everything's fine until somebody wants to discuss something intelligent...in person."

"And then you ignore them," I said.

"Absolutely. Cell phones. Greatest invention on earth. You always say you didn't have it on you." Chris laughed at the absurdity of that one, "Are you kidding me? *Nobody* doesn't keep their cell phone on them anymore. Or it's at least two feet away from them. Not one person leaves their cell phone in their car all day. But you tell 'em that. You didn't have your phone on you. The next time you say your battery died. You didn't have your car charger. You were in a dead zone. For like six hours. You left your charger in your suitcase. You forgot your password. You had the phone on vibrate in a meeting and forgot to turn the sound on. Left it in airplane mode. As if people are not continually checking for messages every five minutes and you would have seen it. But you swear up and down you missed their call somehow."

"And then what do you do when they track you down and they want to have a real conversation?" I asked.

Chris said, "Then you stall. Then you tell them you're like four hours away from them because you had an appointment. Traffic. You're stuck in it. They try to get you to meet 'em later. You're stuck for hours. Horrible traffic jam. California's perfect for *that* story. You try to stall them off until tomorrow. And your cell phone battery is running low and you forgot your car charger. Who takes their car charger out of their car? Or your boss is calling on the other line. Gotta go."

"And if they're still persisting on getting together," Chris continued, "then you gotta dig deep. You pull out the car accident. Some idiot just hit me from behind. It's gonna be *hours* with all this paperwork we have to fill out now. Just not gonna be able to make it tonight. Accident."

Chris explained pre-planning, "But the smart ones plan their alibis early. When you know you're going to be out all night, you check in early with a predetermined alibi, so they won't expect to hear from you for the rest of the night, possibly into the next day. You tell them you're going out of town for work or with your buddy to a game or something, and you already know you don't get reception wherever you're going. You're on a business trip and they lost your luggage with your charger. Obviously no one sells them for nineteen dollars in the city you're in. You forgot to charge your battery before you went to your family's house and it's almost dead. Of course, you never have your charger on you. Somebody else is driving. Your charger's in your car. There can't be any way you could possibly get a battery charged and nobody has landlines anymore. Try to find a pay phone or a mail box these days. These things don't even exist anymore. So you set it up with them knowing that you won't be checking back in until sometime tomorrow."

"My buddy is actually worse than I am," Chris told me. "He likes to go into Tijuana. I guess they have good deals on pottery and leather down there, not to mention dollar tacos. It's worth four hours of gas getting in and out of Tijuana for the dollar tacos. We have to stop before we cross the border so he can make eight or nine texts before we go into the dead reception zone. He's gotta tell eight or nine women different stories about where he's at."

"How does he keep them straight?" I asked.

"He doesn't," Chris laughed. "He was sitting on the couch texting with four or five different women and he tells me, 'Don't you hate it when you've gotta read back ten or twelve comments to see how you're supposed to be responding to whom? You don't know which line to send on which text.' He couldn't remember which lie he'd told each woman, so he was thumbing back through all the previous texts to make sure he had his stories straight."

Chris continued, "We were in a bar one night and he was supposed to go over to some chick's house and this other one who knew him came over and sat down. She got up to go the bathroom and he says to me, 'Let's go.' I asked him, what about what's-her-face? He looks at me and says, 'You've known me for years. You know damn well I don't know her name. Let's get outta here.' So we left."

"Do you ever get lonely or sad?" I asked.

"Not really. Nothing that nine or ten quick drinks couldn't cure," Chris chuckled.

"Can you imagine yourself ever feeling *happy* settling down with one woman?" I inquired. "I think I know the answer to that."

Chris laughed, "It's perfect when you travel a lot. Ideally, you could have several women scattered around in different states that you travel to....and you never have to have a home game."

*I'd like to note: Passive aggression does not imply a man will not be loyal and committed, but it's not uncommon for them to be womanizers.

Your Subconscious Stupidity

Our subconscious mind does not really have a mind of its own. It's a Yes Man. It always takes direction from our conscious mind. Our conscious mind is heavily influenced by our fear. We may say we want something, but we're secretly afraid we won't be able to get it. We want it bad. But we fear we're not capable or worthy of having it.

So our conscious mind tells our mouth to say we want success in love and life, but it really doesn't believe we're capable of attaining it. And whatever our conscious mind secretly *believes* to be true is the direction it gives our subconscious. While we're saying we want success, we're directing our subconscious not to give it to us, because our fear doesn't believe we can have it. Our subconscious mind is the Great Saboteur. It will ensure all of our fears are realized and none of our desires will come to fruition. Here's a typical exchange between our fearful conscious brain and its order-taking subordinate, the subconscious mind:

> *Conscious brain: I'm dying for a great romantic love. I'm afraid I won't find love*
>
> *Subconscious: You won't find love. Trust me*
>
> *Conscious brain: I want my soul mate but I fear I'll never find that kind of love*
>
> *Subconscious: You'll never find love. I'm on it. You won't be lovable*

To be so smart, how can we be so dumb? We've seen the evidence that points to a correlation between *belief* and *attainment*. We hear famous athletes attributing their achievements to visualization tactics. We've heard the success stories from people who achieved the impossible by employing mind-over-matter techniques. But we never apply these techniques to our own lives. We're too busy. We're working long hours at jobs we hate. We're taking care of everyone else but ourselves. We're stewing over things that other people did that upset us. We're putting time, thought, and energy into dysfunctional relationships that don't bring us emotional satisfaction. And when we get a free minute, we sign onto Facebook.

Are We Doomed?

Our society goes through cycles, just like fashion styles repeat themselves. Hip-huggers reemerged as "low-cut" jeans, and the "tree-hugging" hippy movement of the sixties has become the "green" earth-friendly generation.

Many of us have become frustrated with the absence of the human element in our day-to-day lives. We're tired of talking to automated voices. We beg for a "live" person. We're too lazy to get out of our cars so we go through the drive-up window, but then we hold up the line because we love talking to the cashier.

We respect the value the individual brings to our society, rather than dismissing them because their external self doesn't look like us. We elected our first black president named Obama, and chose a member of the Mormon Church to be his opponent. We keenly follow the work of an agnostic physicist and a super-star scientologist.

If you follow astrology, you noted our race through the Age of Aquarius was all about science, brains, and speed. Now we're into the age of Pisces, which is a softer, loving sign.

People are craving human interaction instead of electronic messages. We've stretched technology as far as we want to go towards the elimination of the personal human touch. Connecting with old friends at a high school reunion invigorates us with their old familiar energy in person, while their recent pictures viewed on Classmates did nothing to refresh their spirit in our minds. They were just pictures of another middle aged person who looked vaguely recognizable, but didn't *feel* familiar.

To reconnect with the heart and soul of a person, we must offer our own in exchange. I believe most of us are ready and anxious to do that. After banging our heads against frozen computer screens, groaning over slow connections, and screaming in frustration when our phone only shows one bar; we have a new appreciation for the friend who literally "drops everything and runs" to our assistance. We've finally realized the speed of technology is no substitute for the urgency a human exhibits when we're in distress.

Those of us on dating websites also realize that "the truth" in black and white is not always the truth, and there's no substitute for meeting face-to-face. People doctor their image and lie in their profile hoping to attract someone who "matches" them. And they advertise their fear in bold print.

The guy who wants a partner with "no baggage" chooses "DamagedGoods" as his screen name. The woman who just wants an "honest man" posts pictures that are ten years old.

And as my friend Jim wondered, "Since when did 'a few extra pounds' come to mean a hundred pounds overweight?"

Have people become so accustomed to hiding behind their computer screen that they forget the object of a dating web site is to meet someone in person? And while you're sizing them up over coffee, they are also comparing the *real* you against the distorted illusion you gave them? Authenticity is the key to finding a real match. Projecting a phony image will only increase your fear of being unworthy of the person sipping their java beside you, and that's not exactly the perfect start to a relationship that promotes your own sense of self-worth.

So as we move into the next generation of communications, I have faith in the human species desire to connect with other living souls on real terms. Being "real" means coming from love instead of fear. Fear of being authentic causes the true spirit of the person to become swallowed up in layers of images that have been constructed over the years. Internally, fear has created a hellish funhouse of mirrored distortions of self.

If your own self-image is downgrading while the networking site is uploading, get off the computer!

Stop the Madness

I'm not advocating deleting yourself off of Facebook. In fact, Facebook presented a magnificent life-line to me when I was deep in heavy contemplation for months and my friends were wondering if I had checked out instead of checking in. I could sign on late at night when I had finished my evening self-analysis and post a comment to attest to my continued existence.

But if your self-esteem has been hinging on the popularity of your online persona, then maybe a Facebook break is in order. If you step in your front door and immediately race to your computer to monitor the online activities of others, then you're addicted to worrying about what others think of you. Your self-worth has hit an all-time low and you're desperately trying to define your worth in a box with a 200 character limit. You're stalking the activities of people you envy instead of doing something creative to boost your own self-esteem.

Breaking your addiction to things that cause you pain can be a lot like breaking up. You go through a withdrawal period and you're pacing around trying to find something to occupy yourself with. You suddenly have idle time. Of course, everyone always advocates using that time to start a new health care regimen. We all know that would be the most productive use of our time, and it would make us feel better about ourselves because we'd look better, too. But I'm not going to get on a soap box telling you what you already know, so I'm offering other ideas to help you break-up with the Facebook offenders.

Expand your circle of friends, but don't stop at Facebook. Try Linked-In or any of the pages for non-profit organizations or community outreach programs. There are thousands of open groups on the web. Every type of interest, hobby, religion, or curiosity is represented. Join a discussion group that interests you. Find an online community that shares a fondness for one of your hobbies. There are book clubs, support groups, metaphysical communities, and open discussions for positive thinkers. Best of all, you can find a self-help group for virtually any kind of issue you're grappling with. Misery always loves company, and the web makes it easy to connect with others who are dealing with the same misery. People share stories and tips for coping with every kind of problem imaginable. You'll start making connections with people who are a cut above your regular offenders.

When you make a conscious decision to extract yourself from the pool of negativity that surrounds you, you'll begin gravitating toward higher-level thinkers. You'll find yourself logging onto your computer to check out the latest post from the scientist in your discussion group, rather than the latest jab from your ex best friend.

Start thinking of yourself as "above" the childishness, and take steps to show yourself that you are. Don't concern yourself with how others are viewing your new interests. This is not about them. It's about you.

Treat yourself to an outing at the book store, preferably one with a coffee shop attached. Grab a cup of your favorite brew and peruse the shelves for self-help books on your own brand of crack cocaine. Passive aggression? Commitment-phobia? Eating disorders? Control issues? Stress management? There's something for everyone.

Check out the humor section. Something will catch your eye and you can have a few chuckles while sipping your coffee. Look in the hobbies sections. Is there something you always wanted to learn to do? Feng shui? Home-brewed beer? Gardening? Playing bridge?

Check out the cookbooks. Maybe you've always wanted to learn how to make homemade pasta or tamales.

Bring a small pad of paper and a pen with you to jot stuff down. Unless you have unlimited funds, you can't buy every book that interests you. You can make a list of subject matter that struck your curiosity and then go home and look it up on the web for free.

Spend a few minutes gazing at the incredible selection of tabletop science books. You don't have to be a physicist to appreciate the amazing photos of nebulas and galaxies far, far away. You'll be intrigued with the tidbits of knowledge you glean from science books, and you may decide you'd like to learn more by joining a science discussion group online.

Hit the spiritual/religion section. Don't be off-put if you're not a religious nut. There are hundreds of interesting titles in here, ranging from Chicken Soup books that inspire you, to spiritual books advising you how to attract your soul mate. Jot down some tips from all of them. But bypass the book of witchcraft spells and do-it-yourself-voodoo doll kits. You're *above* that, remember?

Stop by the table of trivia books. These are great sources for creating interesting posts of your own. I love it when my friends post fun facts and interesting trivia on their Facebook walls. Don't want to buy one? Jot down some of your favorite facts. The next time you're tempted to retaliate against the slanderous poster with a vengeful post of your own, stop yourself and pull out your list of fun facts. Instead of getting ignored by your friends or instigating further negative comments, you'll instantly receive positive feedback from people remarking on the curious tidbit. Remember, you're *above* the negativity now.

My favorite sections are psychology and philosophy. Even if you're not affected by abnormal psychological disorders, it's fascinating to read about some of them. Read through some of the new age philosophy books and become familiar with the law of attraction ideology, or the old standbys on positive thinking.

Write down the names of authors whose books you admire. Look them up later on the web. They may have fan pages or discussion groups of their own.

Sports fanatic? Find a book about your favorite player and get inspired by their story of rags-to-riches. Ditto for artists, actors, and musicians.

Wishing you had more friends with these interests? Jot down some fun facts about 70's rock groups or baseball trivia. Post sports trivia on your wall if you want the athletes to comment on your post instead of the gossip girls.

History, geography, anatomy; there are no end of books that may contain strange and interesting facts about our amazing universe. Scan through a couple of paranormal books. Find some weird facts about anything and everything. Jot down some of those.

Do you get the picture? Expand yourself. Start researching things that interest you and you will become more interesting. Keep a list of compelling little tidbits for a rainy Facebook day. Promise yourself you'll use them whenever you're tempted to deliver your own passive aggressive post.

The only thing in the bookstore that's off limits to you besides the voodoo stuff: Tabloids. Tell yourself you are not supporting any publication that prints negativity which is ruining someone *else's* day. You're *above* that. You're out of the gossip chain on a national level.

Go home and clean your house as if you're having company. Why do we always wait to deep clean until we know others are coming over? Clean your house for *you* to enjoy. Give yourself a reward to look forward to. Promise yourself you won't crack open the fascinating new book you bought until your house is sparkling.

Allow yourself indulgences. A bubble bath, candlelight, your favorite CD, an action-adventure movie, a video game, a nap, Kraft macaroni and cheese; whatever you perceive to be a selfish indulgence or luxury.

If you're single and wishing you weren't, then act as if you have a partner. Use the good china, wear something sexy, sleep on one side of the bed instead of in the middle, put on lip gloss or aftershave, *shave!*

Start visualizing the life you want and start behaving as if you're already there, pocketbook permitting. You're tired of being affected by the childish behavior of others? Then start acting like a mature adult who has better things to do than read back-stabbing comments on somebody's Facebook wall. Start developing interests and friendships outside of your normal friend network. You don't have to disconnect with your *real* friends who support you. But your real friends will support your desire to grow up and distance yourself from juvenile behavior.

Write your own mantra for self-worth and self-love, and repeat it numerous times throughout the day. I know you'll feel silly at first, but I promise it helps keep your mind focused on the positive goal of achieving the life you want, instead of the negativity that brings you down. Need some ideas? Here's a short list of general things you might like to add to your mantra, but tailor your own to fit your personal goals:

I am giving and receiving love unconditionally

I am achieving financial prosperity

I am at peace with myself and I forgive others

You can be very specific. I had a finished manuscript for my book, **The Return of Mikey**, but no idea how to begin finding a publisher. I started saying a mantra that included, "I'm getting a publisher and **The Return of Mikey** is being published." I was led to a publisher in less than six months, and my published book was in my hands within a year.

I'm not saying you will get immediate or miraculous results with mantras. But the point of saying a mantra is to focus your mind on positive things so that you will start attracting positive things into your life, instead of attracting more negativity from your negative thinking. You don't hear a basketball player say he visualizes *missing* the free throw. He visualizes the outcome he wants to see. Do the same thing with your mantra. Instead of saying, "I *hope* I make the free throw," make it an affirmative statement. "I am making the free throw."

If you're looking for love, then include that in your mantra. If it's career success you desire, then state your intentions. I used to just recite my mantra up in my head when I was doing other things. You don't need to say it out loud if you're embarrassed. The important thing is that your mind is focused on positive intentions instead of fear.

Practice meditation techniques. You can buy audio tapes that will walk you through a guided meditation.

Spend a quiet moment in prayer or contemplation. If you believe in a higher power, say thank you in advance for helping you to honor your self-worth.

Friend *me* on Facebook or chat with me on my DianeBucci.com page. Send me an email at Diane@DianeBucci.com if you'd like to connect, or follow my affiliate Terryee Abbott at the AngelCoaches community page.

Facebook doesn't cause depression. *We* do. We've become addicted to comparing ourselves to other people. If Facebook is causing you to feel depressed, you need to take a step back and observe yourself for a moment. What do these other people have that you can't get? Big houses, nice vacations, pretty people that surround them? Popularity? Your ex? Let's take a look at these things one by one.

So their house looks nice. Your own living quarters can look equally appealing if you forego the four dollar Starbucks and invest in a few things that give you ambience. If your pocketbook doesn't allow first edition art prints, then hit the Goodwill store or flea markets. Scrounge around for at least one decent wall décor object that speaks to you, and put that on your prominent wall. If four dollars is all you have to spend, go to a Dollar Store and grab a few sprigs of artificial greenery. Here's a tip: you don't have to invest in a pot to put them in. Stuff the stems behind a couple of books on a shelf and spread the ivy leaves out: a ninety-nine cent burst of life suddenly brightens a dark corner. Buy some cheap candles, preferably with a pleasing aroma. If you're allergic to the perfume in candles, then buy the odorless variety. There's nothing like the ambience of candlelight to say, "Special." Clean off your coffee table, desk, orange crate or cinder-block shelf and display your favorite book or magazine next to a ninety-nine cent candle that's nestled into another ninety-nine cent stem of greenery. If you've got an old placemat or scarf, you can swirl the scarf around under your arrangement or display your magazine on top of the placemat. Prop a framed photo next to it. You can instantly create a welcoming ambience for yourself with a minimum of money and a few objects that you may already own.

If you're an avid book reader, display your books. You can stand your books up by propping them open a little bit and spread them across a shelf, arranging them just like a bookstore display with the covers facing out. I've seen several of my friends create an interesting display that filled an entire old bookcase with only nine or ten books. It looks even better if you can add a few more sprigs of greenery amidst the standing books, or a couple of framed photos in the center. And the next time you get the urge for a self-taken photo, position yourself in front of your artfully arranged books, greenery, candles, or wall print. Your picture will look just as good as the one your friend just posted of their kids standing in front of the mansion's fireplace, and you'll feel good about yourself whether you decide to share the picture or not. That's the key point here. You are making yourself feel good about *you*. It doesn't matter what anyone else thinks of you. They're all too worried about how their own images look to be concerned with yours.

Here's another trick to liven up a bedroom wall. Buy some heavy duty push pins and space them out on your wall to display clothing or accessories you already own. You can cover a fairly large area with five or six colorful scarves hanging on the push pins. You can also display necklaces and jewelry like this. My daughter uses the same method in her closet to display evening bags, which are notorious for being slippery little suckers that get lost on closet shelves or buried in drawers. It makes a pretty wall display, since evening bags are usually decorative. You can do the same thing on your bedroom wall with purses or hats or both. Men can make a colorful statement with ties or t-shirts. If you've got five or six t-shirts in different bold colors, hang them on the push pins in a rainbow pattern and liven up a bare dormitory wall. (It also makes it easy to grab one when you're in a hurry to throw on a clean t-shirt and run out the door.)

Listen to the interior decorators and the feng shui experts.   Your surroundings really do make a difference in how you feel and how you perceive yourself. If your home-sweet-home feels boring or depressing, then you need to change it up a little. It will give your mood a lift, and you'll look forward to the time you spend in it, instead of wishing you were living in one of your friends' pictures. And don't stop at the inside. A welcoming front door area will not only look inviting to you, but others as well.

You don't need a big backyard to spruce up the outside of your pad. Skip the movie rentals and buy a potted petunia or a hanging basket to place outside your front door or on your balcony. Find a cheap lawn chair to sit next to it, and you've got an instant little sanctuary for yourself. It's even better if you can position the plant to view when you're inside your home.   A botanical view always makes you feel spoiled, and lifts your spirits when you're feeling either depressed or just poor. Sip your morning coffee while you're lounging in your sunny chair, smelling the fragrance of the petunias instead of checking your friend's Facebook status from the fluorescent glow of a computer screen.

Moving onto those vacation pictures which you're lacking because you haven't been able to afford to take a vacation....you don't need to. You don't have to invest in a trip to Paris to enjoy cultural beauty around you. Grab your camera and take a jaunt down to the closest museum or city park. If you can't afford to buy the museum admission ticket, there are plenty of statues, sculptures, and free botanical gardens around your closest city center. When we marvel at the beauty in our friends' vacation photos, we're admiring architecture and nature. These things are free all around you. Historical sites are always interesting and we've all got some in our own backyard. But you have to get away from your computer to find them. Ask your best friend to join you for a walk in your neighborhood and make it your mission to find as many funny or unusual photo ops as you can. Call your mom and invite her to a day in the park or a community sponsored garden in the city. Pack a picnic lunch along with your camera and you'll have amazing photo-ops with someone who *knows* you are the greatest person who ever lived. Moms will always attest to that. The Eiffel Tower can't compare to your mom in front of a naked statue, or your dad in front of the monkey cage at the zoo. You don't need an ocean for water pictures. Everybody has a pond or two near them with a couple of ducks on it. Mountains are beautiful, but so is a close-up of a perfectly formed dandelion.

Take mom or dad or your kid to that cool little restaurant you always wanted to try. Ungrateful girlfriends and boyfriends will come and go, but your family will never forget the memory, and you'll never have to delete the picture. You don't need to post your mini "vacation" pictures. They're for you to enjoy and experience. But if you want something besides self-taken bathroom photos on your page, then by all means post them.

Next up: pretty people pictures. Are you really ogling their physical beauty, or are you envious of their happy expressions? Nothing beats a picture of a loved one laughing. They don't need to look like a movie star. In fact, some movie stars don't *look* like movie stars. So while you're taking your mini vacation in the park with your best friend or family member, snap lots of shots of mom laughing at the nude bronze man she's got her arm around, or your best friend cracking up at a joke, or your kid's expression with the big ice cream cone in front of his face. Or your dog who is chewing your ninety-nine cent greenery back at the ranch.

How about that popularity thing? Have you noticed that some of the most popular, interesting people rarely go on Facebook? They don't have time to sit in front of a computer. They're guys who are skiing instead of friending. They're women who are breaking a sweat in yoga class instead of checking out status columns. They're best friends and spouses enjoying the comedy club together instead of commenting on each other's posts for the twenty-fifth time that day. So instead of "friending" people who are not really your friends in order to have a huge "friends" list, why not start telling yourself you're too busy enjoying life to spend more time at a computer? Whatever your mind believes is what you will put out there to other people. If your subconscious believes you're pathetic and friendless, that's the message you will express to the universe. But if you convince your subconscious that you're just too busy enjoying life to have time corresponding with acquaintances on Facebook, that's the message you'll start sending out to everyone else. The trick is to make your conscious mind believe this first, and you can do that by *making* yourself too busy to stay at home on the computer. Once again, you don't need funds. You just need a plan every night. Which one of your real friends has free time to hang out with you on any particular night? Make a list of all the places you can visit within walking distance, and set a weekly schedule to check out the latest selection at the video store, or the recent additions to the neighborhood playground, or one of the many walking trails that may be around you. Make appointments with yourself to visit the cultural exhibits within driving distance, and promise you'll at least take *yourself* into that cool little restaurant for a cup of coffee with a newspaper in hand. When you get out and about, you'll be amazed at the interesting people you actually do meet and make friends with. Real friends with common interests; not fake Facebook friends who share links.

Lastly, we come to your ex. This is worthy of an entire chapter in itself, so let's continue this onto the next page.

Stop Stalking your Ex

Since the stalking of lovers and *ex*-lovers seems to be a favorite past-time of many Facebook users, it begs for inclusion in this book. I think of it as your very own passive aggressive way to hurt *yourself*.

> "He just friended a woman from Boise. I checked out her page and she doesn't have a boyfriend. I'm afraid he's cheating on me with her. I read all her posts and I *hate* her."

Well, for starters, there must be something wrong in *your* relationship if you immediately become suspicious of cheating just because your partner has a new friend who is the same sex as you are. A third party is never the cause of a problem between romantic partners. If there is an existing problem, a third party is just as escape route for one of them. Don't blame the third party. Look within the relationship between the *two* of you to determine the problem. The problem may just exist in one of the partners. They may be afraid of commitment to *anyone*, or they may have other extenuating circumstances that prohibit their desire to carry the relationship to a more serious level. Maybe they want to move to a different state, and they don't want to get any more attached to you. Maybe they can tell you're expecting a serious commitment and they're just not ready to settle down. Or maybe you're a jealous leach and you're driving them away. Ever think of that? Maybe a loyal partner has become weary of being accused of cheating just because they have friends who are both men and women. And no matter how much they try to prove they're trustworthy, your suspicion suffocates them like the heavy cloak of the grim reaper and they're freaking tired of it. And *yes*, that woman in Boise will be the next person they pursue, as soon as they dump *your* insecure ass.

> "Guess who has a new boyfriend now? I saw it on her Facebook wall. I stalked him and he's Mr. Perfect, of course. He's got every toy I always dreamed of having, huge house, great job, smart kids, and he looks like he should be in a GQ ad."

You mean you didn't have a butcher knife handy to twist into your own gut? Damn, you gotta be more prepared next time you want to self-mutilate.

> "I noticed he posted new vacation pictures. He actually took that trip that he was supposed to go on with me! Can you believe that? We talked about it for two years and I can't believe he went without me."

You thought his world stopped the same moment yours did? Did you realize you're the one who is holding the stop-watch?

The only thing stalking your ex will do is keep you stuck in that moment of misery. You can't move on until you let go of the past, and reminding yourself of a painful break-up will only keep that wound from healing. Why do you think he posted those vacation pictures? It may have been a passive aggressive way

116

to rub your nose in his independence. He may also carry a grudge and he hopes to hurt you from afar.

He may be a callous person who is so intent on advertising his big vacation that he doesn't care if it hurts you. If that's the case, then look at his motives for self-promotion. He feels insecure with himself and he's trying to make his life look exciting regardless of who he hurts. Do you want a partner who chooses feeding his own fragile ego over sparing someone else pain?

Lastly, he may not even realize you care enough to stalk his page, and it may not have occurred to him that his vacation pictures would bother you. Maybe you've been an exceptional actress and your ex really believes he's out of your sight and your mind. If so, good for you! But now you've got to believe your own acting job.

But let's back up and ponder his possible motives for wanting to hurt you. The Revenge factor. He wouldn't put energy into "getting even" if he didn't feel he was wronged by you. Instead of getting angry at him, look at your own behavior and determine what you might have done or said that would have given him the urge to get even. Get even for what? His perspective is obviously different from yours. He is looking at you and saying, "You did something to hurt me." His hurt feelings may be justified, although he may be employing immature tactics to express them by enacting revenge. If he was the one who decided to end the relationship, he had reasons that prompted him to do so. Don't cop out and blame another love interest for stealing him away from you. Either your relationship wasn't giving him everything he desired or he may be someone who doesn't want to be tied down to anyone for a long length of time. He's just playing the field and wants to advertise his independence. You might not have said anything derogatory about him to provoke him. His interest in promoting his solo vacation may have been strictly a personal desire to express his freedom to the world. But if you believe he was purposely trying to hurt you, you need to realize that in order for him to *feel* vengeful, there had to be something you did or said that offended his ego or wounded his heart at some point. So take a look at his underlying motivations instead of taking it personal.

If you were the one who chose to end the relationship, you might not have done anything to hurt him *except* hurting his feelings by breaking it off with him in an honest, mature fashion. But he is hurt because he didn't want the relationship to end, and he's blaming you for the pain he's feeling. There is nothing you can do to justify yourself to him. He's experiencing the pain of breaking up, and people deal with it in different ways. Revenge is, unfortunately, a common reaction.

Part of becoming an adult is learning how to stifle the urge to get revenge when you've been hurt. You only prolong the agony by taking turns doing the eye-for-an-eye routine. You get back at them, and then they get back at you for what you did to get back at them, and then you get back at them for that, and it continues ad nauseam. So if you believe your ex is posting things out of revenge, then take the high road and ignore it. Take the self-preservation road, and stop stalking them.

Why do we feel compelled to keep trying to connect with someone who no longer wants us in their life? Why do our physical bodies seem to crave that person we lost?

Barbara Ann Brennan was a research scientist for NASA, and says she began seeing auras around things in nature when she was young. Trees, small animals, everything has an aura around it that is larger than its physical body. She realized all these auras, or energy bodies were connected. Everything around us is connected with invisible energy. Barbara became interested in the human energy field, and eventually built her own business as a healing practitioner. Barbara can see the energy fields of people, and she sees cords of energy connecting them to other people. People who have love between them are literally connected through their heart chakras with these cords, the basis for the phrase "heart strings." The greater and deeper the love, the stronger and greater the number of energy cords connecting them.[2]

When a relationship is ended, those energy connections, or heart strings, get severed. People who see auras describe the rejected lover's energy field as looking like an octopus with tentacles trying to reattach themselves to the lost partner. Those heart strings are flailing around in space, looking for someone to reattach themselves onto. But rebounding, or attempting to reattach onto a new person will not have the same connection, because it's not the same energy source as the previous partner who created those energy cords. People who can see these auras describe the healing process appearing as if those octopus tentacles gradually grow back into the person. You must grow your heart strings back into yourself before you will finally feel normal and healed again. That's the metaphysical explanation for why you feel like you just lost part of yourself when you get cut loose by someone you love. You feel lost and aimless. You don't feel normal. Your body feels literally sick. It's like a part of you is suddenly missing, because in a way, it is. Your energy body doesn't have those connecting strands that were latched on to your partner. You are that octopus, flailing around trying to find your old partner.

So it's not just the absence of viewing your ex in person or hearing their voice that you miss, but you are suddenly feeling the absence of their energy body that connected with your heart chakra. You have to allow yourself time to heal and let your heart strings grow back into you, instead of attempting to rebound onto a new person. It doesn't just happen overnight, as we would like.

The problem that arises when you're continually viewing your ex online is that you're constantly trying to reconnect with their energy while you're gazing at pictures of their physical being, and I believe it slows your healing process. As hard as it may be to refrain from checking out their Facebook page, it's better if you can force yourself not to do it. You're only prolonging your own agony, and postponing the ability to feel "normal" again. Often, viewing pictures of the smiling face of your ex also brings hurt feelings up to the surface again, as well as anger or resentment.   Constantly refreshing the raw open wound with more negative emotions is not conducive to healing and moving forward to happier times, in spite of your flailing tentacles that are desperate to behold your ex.

So while the word "stalking" usually sounds like you're doing something despicable to someone *else*, you're truly hurting *yourself* if you're stalking someone on the internet who severed ties with you. I always ask people who are lamenting the loss of a love, "Do you really want that person back, or do you just want to feel happy again?"   Sometimes we convince ourselves that the lost love would make us instantly happy if they were to reappear in our life, so we replay a recording over and over that says how much we want them back. But what we really want is to just feel happy. We're setting a roadblock up in front of ourselves when we say we need that particular person in order to feel happy. It's not true. We were happy before we met them, and we can be happy again. But if we tell ourselves we can't feel happy without them, then we won't be. That's the command we're giving our subconscious.

What if you are the one who gravitates toward those relationships which can't blossom into a full-blown commitment or even a publicly recognized romance? I've been there myself, but didn't realize it at the time.

My ex-husband and I were married for twenty years, and we parted very amicably. I had gotten married at such a young age, I basically had gone from my parent's house to my husband's; with a brief stop in an apartment I shared with a roommate in college. I had never really been on my own.

So after the marital separation, I felt the need to keep myself out of the dating game and learn how to stand on my own two feet. I didn't date for several years. When I finally decided I was ready to reengage myself with another man, I began seeing a man who lived in another state. After that relationship ended, I took up with another man who lived in a different state. And yet *another* long-distance romance followed that one. When the third relationship ended, I began doing a lot of internal reflection and realized I had subconsciously chosen men who couldn't place normal expectations on me or the relationship. I really *wasn't* ready to be involved with someone else. I secretly evaded anyone who wanted to have a normal, close relationship that logistically had the potential to blossom into something more serious. I entered into relationships where there was already a predetermined stop; a limit on the amount of time we could spend together, an unavoidable separation that prohibited daily physical interaction, an unspoken reason why the man couldn't make demands on my time.

Upon my realization, I decided to start making a conscious decision to only pursue men who lived near me. I wanted to make myself more available to a partner who was also available to me. I met a man who lived ten miles away from me, and began dating him. But guess what? I soon realized this man wasn't emotionally available to forge a committed relationship with me. He had been through hell with a previous partner and other personal tragedies, and he was not in a place where he could be a whole partner to someone else. He needed time alone to heal from his own wounds, so there was already an invisible stop in place. We could only grow to a certain degree of closeness, and then he would withdraw from me. Our relationship was never allowed to do a natural progression.

After that relationship ended, I had to examine myself once again. I obviously hadn't come as far as I thought I had. Even though I had chosen a man who logistically appeared to be able to have a normal, healthy relationship with me, I was attracted to a man who was clearly not ready to develop one and foster its growth.

Back to square one. I had deceived *myself.* I certainly can't blame the man. He was doing what he needed to do for *himself.* He knew he needed time to decompress from the emotional trauma he had been through, and he never made any promises about "being ready" at some point in the future for a commitment. He was very honest and upfront about the fact that he needed time on his own and he didn't know if he would ever be able to make a major commitment to someone else. He'd been taking care of everyone else for years, and he knew he deserved to finally put his own needs first. He made no apologies for the amount of space he put between us. It was a take-it-or-leave-it deal, and he didn't beg me to stay in that loosely bound relationship with him. In fact, he told me many times that he wouldn't blame me if I walked away from it. In his words, "I wouldn't put up with me either. You deserve better."

And naturally, he used passive aggressive ways of putting distance between us. He avoided telephone conversations with me like the plague. He cancelled out on plans at the last minute, and always had an excuse for why we couldn't spend more time together. He ignored texts, phone calls, and brushed off my attempts to get together. Once again, I found myself "in a relationship" that wasn't really a relationship. It was a series of dates; some of which lasted several days, but did not bring us closer together. I was having a relationship with myself. I was doing all the work to foster a loving bond, and he was being elusive. But, he was being honest.

Another eye-opening moment finally occurred for me. Subconsciously, I wasn't allowing myself to get the kind of love I dreamed of having. By hanging onto a partner who couldn't return my affection and didn't share my desire to grow closer, I was denying myself the relationship I desperately wanted. My fear had kicked in. I wanted that great love in my life so badly that I was attracting what I feared most: the lack of getting it.

Facebook: The Greatest Passive Aggressive Weapon EVER

Living in the Moment

Yes, it sounds cliché, but I want you to take a different look at what "the moment" means to you. When you're happy in your present moment, you're full of positive vibes. Positive attracts more positive. If you feel happy in your present situation and you have a positive outlook on your future, you're essentially saying to yourself, "This moment will be repeated. I am happy right now, so I will be happy five minutes from now. In five minutes I will assume that I will still be happy in another five minutes." Those five minute intervals quickly turn into hours, and then days, and then years.

So it is extremely important for you to fully embrace and feel happy in your current moment in order to attract more happiness in the future. The ability to feel absolutely content and joyful in our present state is the monster that we all struggle with. It's a wrestling match between our desire to be happy and our fear that we won't be. Fear always wins if we let it. If we say to ourselves, "I feel joyful in my current moment but I'm afraid it won't last," then we sabotage ourselves. We'll cause the fear to come to fruition.

I dated a man who used to say, "I love you so much. This is the relationship I always dreamed of but never thought possible. I'm so afraid I'm going to fuck it up." Do I need to tell you that, yes; he did everything humanly possible to *fuck it up*?

Listen very closely to the words that come out of your own mouth. You're essentially placing an order with the universe. If you say, "I'm afraid I'm going to screw this one up," then you're telling yourself and the world, "I'm going to screw this one up."

People who say, "I'm afraid I'm going to get fired," are giving their subconscious the command, "I'm going to get fired." They will subconsciously begin sabotaging their own performance at work.

If you say, "I don't know if I can step up to the plate," your fear is telling you that you may not be able to accomplish what you want. So the order you're placing with your subconscious is, "I can't step up to the plate."

Then there are those fear-based questions that slide out of our mouths all the time. "Why isn't she calling? How come she never calls?" Universal energy translation: "She isn't calling. She never calls." The universe always returns what we expect. If our fear expects disappointment, the universe returns in kind.

It's difficult, and yes at times impossible, to feel content every moment. Make a conscious effort to mentally acknowledge your gratitude for the positive things in your life, even when things are bad. There are always things we can be thankful for. Maybe you lost your job and your girlfriend, but you still have your mom and your dog. Make a mental thank-you note for Mom and Fluffy.

My son, Mikey, was autistic and his "socially unacceptable" behavior demanded my time and attention. I always felt guilty that my daughter, Susie, had to take the back seat out of necessity quite often. As Mikey matured, he became cognizant of his own behavior. He was a highly functioning individual and he had great compassion for others. While Mikey's disorder gave others the impression that he was self-absorbed, he was actually keenly intuitive when it came to human relations.

Susie became immersed in a very intensive high school marching band program, and since Mikey no longer monopolized my time, I threw myself into supporting Susie by being an active band-mom. I didn't miss a practice, a ball game, or a concert. I was an ever-present fixture on the sidelines, with camcorder, pom-poms, and Mikey in tow. Not only did I *want* to be there because I enjoyed watching Susie and her band, but I knew owed it to her. I felt horrible knowing she'd taken a back seat to her younger brother for most of her life, although I never verbalized that feeling to Mikey. But I didn't have to.

One day I had to pull Mikey away from a movie he'd just started watching, because I wanted to make it to a band show on time. I realized I had been dragging him away from his own activities every day in order to accompany me. I apologized to Mikey, who had been a sport the entire band season; never complaining about giving up much of his free time to go watch band practice with me. Most teenage boys would have loudly objected. But Mikey simply shrugged with patient acceptance, and replied with the intuitive wisdom of an old soul, "I hogged all your attention when I was little and I acted like a hellion. It's Susie's turn now."

When I lost Mikey shortly after his twenty-fifth birthday, I struggled to keep my focus on positive things. If I felt a self-pity party coming on when I was missing Mikey, I said a little prayer of thanks for still having Susie in my life. And when I got so low that it was difficult to feel gratitude for the hand I'd been dealt, Mikey's own words would echo in my mind. "It's Susie's turn now." I would instantly feel grateful that I had the ability to drop everything to show up for my daughter when she needed me, wanted me, or simply tolerated me.

The moral of the story is that no matter how terrible you think your life is or what kind of tragedy you're faced with, you *always* have something to feel grateful for. Acknowledge it. Focusing on something positive gives your energy an immediate lift, and helps attract more positive energy into your life. Focusing on the negative and painful aspects of your life will only keep you trapped in that oppressive state of misery, and attract more misery.

When you feel inclined to stalk the pages of people you envy, people who've hurt you, or people you wish you had a connection with; hit the pause button and imagine Mikey is whispering in your ear, "It's *your* turn now." Be kind to *yourself*. And if your lights happen to flicker while you're imagining that whispered urging, then take that as a sign that Mikey isn't whispering. He's yelling at you.

Of course, special days are always tough when you're dealing with the loss of a person or relationship, and you often find yourself traipsing back down memory lane. After losing my son shortly before the holidays four years ago, I was surprised to discover I dreaded New Year's Day as intensely as I had dreaded Christmas without Mikey. For some reason, the clock turning over to a new year seemed incomprehensible. It was as if Mikey's death had suddenly become "a thing of the past," while my grief was still excruciatingly raw in the present. I didn't want a new year to begin; a year which Mikey would never be a part of. I didn't want to start saying, "He died in 2008," as if time had already healed my freshly wounded heart and I could reference his life as if I was talking about my senior prom; as if it was just a part of previous years gone by.

Death and break-ups can be very similar in some ways. While losing a child is the most horrific loss I've ever faced, I have experienced lingering pain from losing loves in romantic break-ups which rivaled my lingering pining for Mikey. I'm not saying a romantic break-up remotely resembles the pain of losing a loved one to death, but losing a relationship with someone you love is one of the most painful ordeals in life, no matter how that loss is incurred.

Special days always bring memories of the previous years when you celebrated them, and those memories can become daggers tearing through a heart that's already hemorrhaging. Often times, it's not the memories themselves, but the absence of memories that were *supposed* to have been created. It may come in the form of presents that you had carefully selected and lovingly wrapped for that person, which are still sitting there unopened. Or the plans for the vacation you had already made with that person which will never come to fruition.

Whether your loss is through death or break-up, your mind becomes filled with shoulda, coulda, woulda's. Even more painfully, you have all the, "We were supposed to's."

> *We were supposed to go camping this summer, or go to Paris next year, or go to the ballgame next weekend. I wonder if he's there with her. We were supposed to get married after she finished school. We were supposed to go skiing over Christmas break. I wonder if she went with her new boyfriend. We were supposed to live happily ever after. I wonder if she looks happy without me.*

And then you have the "I had already gotten's."

> *I had already gotten us tickets for that, or gotten his birthday present, or gotten a loan for her surgery. I had already gotten a new dress to wear to the formal with him.*

Rounding out those thoughts, you have the "I promised" or "They promised" statements.

I promised Mikey I would take him fishing with our new poles on my next weekend off. He had strung the line on the poles and carefully tied the weights and hooks on them after our shopping excursion to his favorite sporting goods store. I can still see him sitting on the couch, patiently tucking my hook around my pole so I wouldn't get pricked. My pole was the pink one. When I absent-mindedly ran my hand across it months after he died, I felt a murderous stab of anguish in my gut that literally doubled me over in pain.

Sudden flashes of "I promised" memories bring you right down to your knees. And then haltingly, the sobs come. Your insides are knotted up so tight that you can't seem to get your lungs to expand to catch a breath in between. Your body seems frozen mid-sob, with no sound coming from you, no ability to breathe, and a frozen expression of agony threatens to permanently contort your face. You lay there in a crumpled heap until the tears make your face raw and the guttural moans have reduced themselves to random hiccupped whimpers. And then you slowly realize you're freezing cold, shivering on the floor of the garage where you're still clutching the pink fishing pole. We were supposed to go fishing on my next weekend off. I promised.

These are the private moments of hell that we all go through when we are grieving the loss of a loved one, whether through death or break-up. While you can't refrain from acknowledging mental reminders of special days, you can refrain from torturing yourself by spending three hours at the computer scrutinizing the latest Facebook postings of the person you're missing on that special day. It will only make you miss them more. It will elevate your private pity-party into a raging extravaganza of emotional agony.

It's impossible to keep your mind focused on the positives in the present moment at times, but you do have the ability to stop that negative thought before it takes over all rational behavior. Whenever your ex pops into your mind, congratulate your brain for being so adept at storing that information for you and pulling it out of the rolodex to remind you to cry. And then tell your brain you're too busy to attend to that thought and you can't waste time stalking your ex at the moment.

Who is the Person Behind Your Profile?

Breaking your addiction to worrying about your image requires you to become acquainted with the real you. When you're coming from a place of authenticity, your outer self is in alignment with your internal being. There's no conflict of interest. Your ego isn't begging to wear a mask to the masquerade ball. You feel confident showing up dressed as yourself, without a costume.

I gauge my own authenticity with people by asking myself, "Would I want this person next to me when I'm sick or depressed?" If the answer is, "No, I have to be on my best game when I see this person," then I know I'm not truly being authentic with them. I only let them see the best parts of me; the me with hair done, make-up on, and a smile to complete the outfit. I will never let them see me down or depressed or grungy. I don't want them at my kitchen table when I wake up with bed-head and morning breath. I will rarely let them see me cry. I'll move mountains before I will allow them a glimpse of my weaknesses. That's not authentic. But the older I get, the more authentic I've become. I don't have one friend on my "friends list" that I'd feel uncomfortable being myself with. I wouldn't call them a friend if I didn't feel free to expose all my warts to them, and I wouldn't be their friend if they couldn't do the same with me.

With age comes self-acceptance. In fact, the ability to feel comfortable in your own skin is quite possibly the only thing of beauty that comes with aging. But it *is* beautiful to look at the crow's feet in the mirror and know there's the heart of a loyal retriever beating beneath the mask of an old crow. Those flabby arms peeking out from the short sleeves of a summer dress have held many a loved one, and embraced a thousand friends with joy. The shoulders, once rigid and erect, have developed a slightly sagging look, but they're still sturdy enough to shoulder a loved one's tears. Buckets of them.

Being a real friend means being authentic and letting your love shine outward, instead of being stingy with crumbs of affection which you're greedily clutching behind the image you've erected. Loving yourself means forgiving yourself for your frailties. Your friends do. If you saw yourself in some of the Offenders, rest assured, your friends saw you before you did. And they still love you anyway. However, they might love you more if you stopped holding up your distorted funhouse mirror for them to view themselves in.

When you truly feel unconditional love for someone, you love qualities in them that you love in yourself. They're holding up a mirror to your best character traits and reflecting them back onto you.

So look at the people you're close to, and define what kind of reflection that offers you. Drama and volatility or tranquility and stability? Secrets and lies or openness and honesty? Loyalty or betrayal? You've drawn these people into your life for a reason. If they are not reflective of the real you, then maybe you chose them to teach you a lesson. It's so important to realize you don't "attract all the losers." You are attracted *to* them. You bring people into your life for a reason. Don't hate the teacher just because their class is hard. Sometimes they're the best teachers. You won't need to repeat the class again with another teacher, although you may decide to break-up with the mean teacher.

You don't need to break-up with Facebook. But you'll be much happier if you begin grooming your inner beauty as much as you tweak your profile page. You're never too old to ask yourself, "Who am I and who do I aspire to be?" If you start aspiring to be your authentic self, the rest comes easy. You weren't created with all this tarnish around your silver lining. God didn't originally craft you as a jealous, insecure, spiteful soul. You've acquired those qualities over a lifetime, and perhaps many lifetimes. When you start making yourself feel good about being *you*, you'll stop allowing your fear to feed your addiction to crafting the image that others view. And you won't even care if they "like" it.

Credits

[1] Lynne Namka, Ed. D, The Boomerang Relationship; Passivity, Irresponsibility and Resulting Partner Anger, as printed in Talk, Trust, and Feel Therapeutics, 1998

[2] Barbara Ann Brennan, Hands of Light; A Guide to Healing Through the Human Energy Field. Bantam Books, 1987

About the Author:

Diane Bucci is the author of **The Return of Mikey**, Irwin Award winner for "Most Inspirational Book of the Year 2012."   Diane is a motivational speaker, private spiritual coach, and avid Facebook user.

Inquiries to: Diane@DianeBucci.com